Metal Clay Magic

Making silver jewelry the easy way

Nana V. Mizushima

Contents

To my parents, Yoneko and Masataka, who introduced me firsthand to the cultures, music, and arts of the world, and to the memory of my friend Michiko Sugano, who had a wonderful enthusiasm for life.

Printed in the United States of America

05 06 07 08 09 10 11 12 13 14   10 9 8 7 6 5 4 3 2

Publisher's Cataloging-In-Publication
(Prepared by The Donohue Group, Inc.)

Mizushima, Nana V.
  Metal clay magic : making silver jewelry the easy way / Nana V. Mizushima.

   p. : ill. ; cm.
  ISBN: 0-87116-220-2

1. Jewelry making. 2. Precious metal clay. 3. Silver jewelry. 4. Silverwork. I. Title.

TT212 .M59 2005
739.27

Senior art director: Lisa Bergman

Book design: Kelly Katlaps, LuAnn Haas Williams

Editors: Julia Gerlach, Terri Torbeck

Photography: Process photos by Nana Mizushima; lead and cover photos by Bill Zuback and Jim Forbes unless otherwise noted.

introduction

Creativity is a fundamental drive we all have—from mechanics to mothers, poets to physicists, we need to balance our busy lives with purely creative, joyful expression. The variety of metal clay products now available are wonderfully suited to helping us obtain this goal.

Metal clay (fine silver and gold you can mold with your hands!) has opened the door to what has previously been an intense and demanding art form—metal work. This new way of working with precious metal allows people of all backgrounds and skill levels to enjoy creating fine silver pieces. But many professional jewelers and craftspeople are also excited by the new possibilities this material offers.

This introductory book provides you with the basics for getting acquainted with metal clay without investing in expensive equipment and lengthy coursework. As a non-metalsmith myself, I can appreciate the desire to simply get your hands on this material and DO IT! Here, I provide you with the essential information and tips you can use right away to get started. Many of the basic tools and equipment are already in your home. If you follow the lessons in this guide, you should have a finished piece within the day! You can go as far as you want in this medium. Keep it simple and basic or intricate and innovative—it is up to you! No matter your style, I'm sure you too will find metal clay to be fun and easy to work with.

My other career is in international education and student advising, so I approach metal clay as a means by which people can satisfy their life goals. I hope that you will enjoy my introduction to these products and embark upon a satisfying and fun adventure. This book will show you the first steps, and then you can decide what you would like to do with them. Start with an easy project to become familiar with the clay; before you know it, you'll be hooked!

Good luck and enjoy creating!

– Nana Mizushima

What is so special about metal clay?

Metal clays, known by the brand names Precious Metal Clay (PMC) and Art Clay Silver, represent an exciting development in precious metals. Developed by Japanese scientists in 1991, metal clay consists primarily of pure silver (or gold) in tiny particles smaller than 20 microns (for perspective, the diameter of a human hair is about 50 microns). These particles are mixed in an organic binder and water formula. During firing, the binder burns away and the precious metal particles sinter, leaving just the precious metal which can be hallmarked as .999 silver or 24K gold. When I began working with metal clay, I immediately focused on the characteristics which make it an ideal medium for expressing creativity.

Metal clay possesses four main characteristics—it is fun, forgiving, fast, and friendly!

Fun—The learning curve for metal clay is a gentle country drive rather than a terrifying roller coaster ride. Start with very simple techniques. Each step is fun, and you have the satisfaction of immediately creating pieces to wear and enjoy. There are many ways to work with metal clay—molding, carving, sanding, extruding, rolling, stamping, texturing, wrapping, folding, cutting, printing . . . and the list goes on. You are only limited by your imagination!

Forgiving—At almost every stage of working with metal clay, you can change your mind or fix mistakes. At the wet clay stage, if you do not like what you have, you can simply roll it up and start over. Any unused metal clay can be stored at room temperature and will not "go bad." If the piece has dried, you can still chop it up and add water to restore it to its clay form. It is wonderfully easy to repair and alter at this dry stage. Even if you have already fired the piece, you have several choices for making changes. I keep a box of odd fired pieces that may be added later to other pieces and refired. I can repair or alter the piece and fire it again. If I dislike the piece, I can sell it to a silversmith. It is .999 fine silver at this point and can be handled as traditional fine silver.

Fast—The original metal clays had to be fired for long periods at a high temperature only sustainable in specially designed electric kilns. The most recent low-fire clays can be fired at 1435°F/780°C for 5 minutes! Low-fire clays can also be fired with a butane torch (like those used for crème brûlée) or in the portable, inexpensive Hot Pot® kiln. Since you can mold metal clay with simple tools and there is no need to pickle (the process of removing oxidation that's done in traditional silversmithing) the finished metal-clay piece, the entire process from start to finish can be a matter of minutes rather than hours or days.

Friendly—Metal clay is not toxic. (It conforms to ASTM D4236.) The most dangerous aspects are the high temperatures of the kilns and torches. In a world full of pollutants and health hazards, it is nice to not have to worry about the effects of metal clay on you and your family's well being. If you educate yourself on the different techniques, tools, and materials which can be used with metal clay, you can work safely. Visit the web sites listed on page 125 regularly for the latest information on metal clay and how different artisans take care of their work environments and their health.

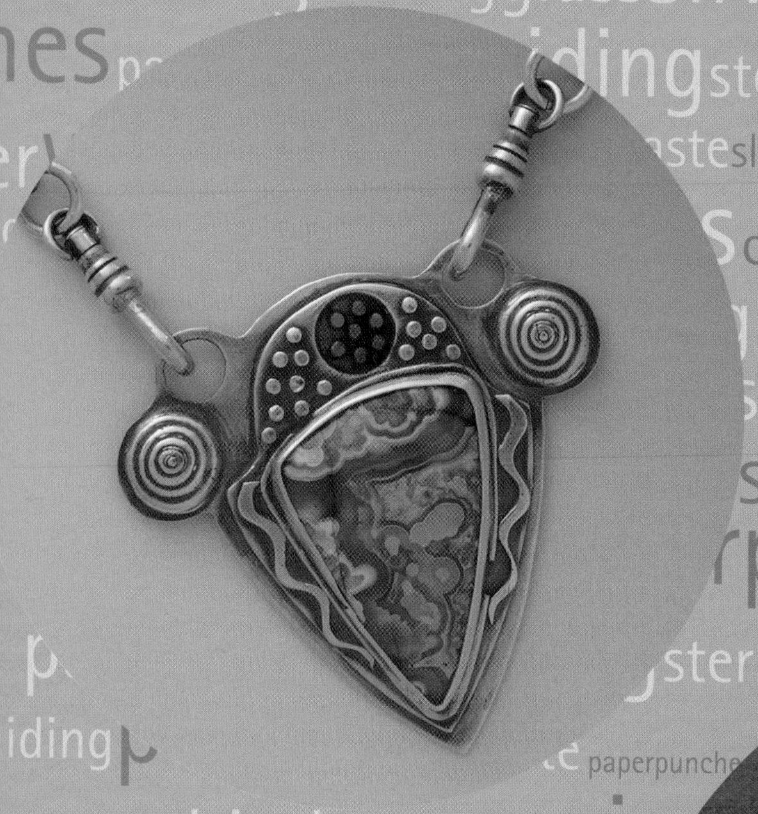

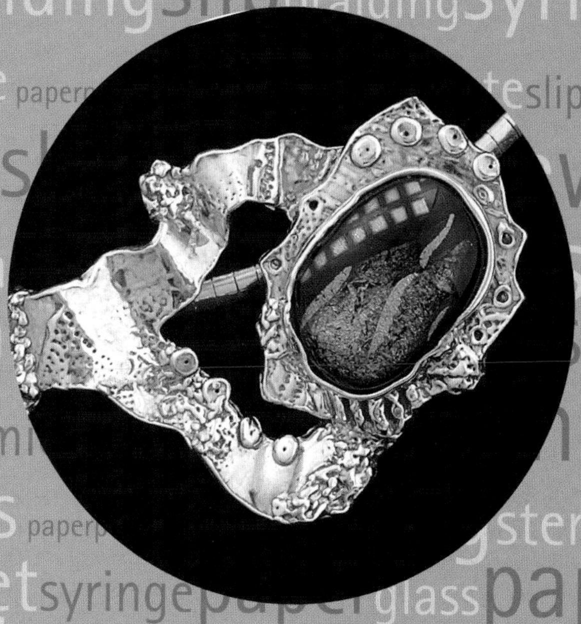

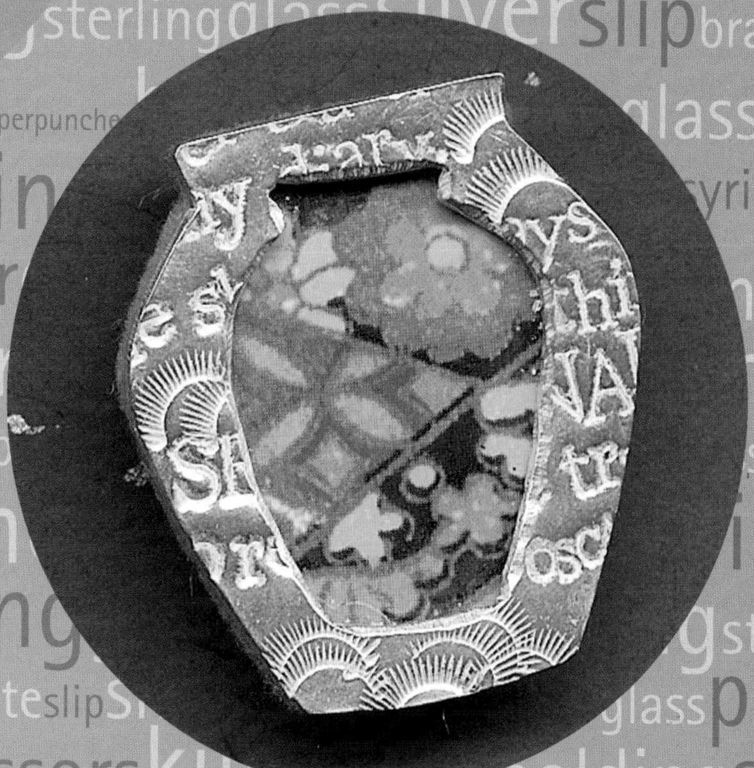

Tools and materials

Traditional silver work involves hundreds of dollars worth of equipment and requires a large space for working with the bulky tools. Metal clay allows you to create in your own home because the tools are simple, small, and inexpensive. The following chapter introduces you to the basic tools required for metal clay work along with the most commonly used metal clay products.

If you want the stimulation of working with others and sharing ideas, you may want to take a class. Check the Education page of the PMC Guild and Art Clay World web sites for current class listings, or find a class at a bead or craft store near your home.

Most important of all, relax and enjoy the process. Working with metal clay can be soothing. And it's fun!

Clockwise from upper right: Pendant slide with dichroic glass by Hattie Sanderson, Speedy Peacock photo; Urn pin by Nana Mizushima, Nana Mizushima photo; Mexican shield with Mexican crazy lace agate by Linda Warner, Linda Warner photo.

Introducing the metal clays

Two manufacturers of metal clay offer a variety of formulas, each of which has distinctive characteristics.

PMC (Precious Metal Clay) products, which include Standard PMC, PMC+, and PMC3, are manufactured by Mitsubishi Materials in Japan.

Art Clay products are produced by Aida Chemical Industries in Japan and include Art Clay Slow Dry, Art Clay Lowfire Silver Overlay Paste, and Art Clay 650.

The two types of metal clay are very similar to handle and comparable in firing temperatures and finishing requirements. Both manufacturers produce clay, paste or slip, paper or sheet, and syringe versions. Most of the techniques and projects in this book can be done with either brand. Both have been available in Japan through retail stores for several years, while in the U.S. they are mainly sold on-line or by telephone. (See "Resources and suppliers," page 125 for distributors.) Pay attention to the weight as well as the price when shopping around. Metal clay is still relatively new and new products are always being developed, so check the manufacturer's web sites or metal clay suppliers for updates.

On the next page, you'll find descriptions of the most commonly used formulas. See the Metal Clay Firing Chart on p. 10 for more information on more the formulas.

PMC3®
The newest version of the PMC line. The biggest advantages are that it:
• can be fired with the portable Hot Pot kiln or a handheld butane torch
• is denser and stronger than the other PMC formulas
• can be fired with enamel, glass, some gemstones, and sterling silver findings. (Some of these added elements require that the piece be fired in a programmable kiln.)

PMC Sheet®
Also known as PMC+ Paper, this type is very different from the lump clay forms. PMC sheet is a thin, flexible sheet which has the following characteristics:
• it remains flexible and does not dry out
• it can be folded
• it can be cut with scissors or paper punches
• it must be fired from a cold kiln in a programmable electric kiln.

Aura 22®
A creamy paste of 22K gold from Mitsubishi Materials that allows you to apply gold directly to fine-silver pieces.

PMC3® Syringe type
Packaged in a ready-to-use syringe, this is 9g of PMC3 slip ready to extrude. A variety of tips are available separately to produce lines of different thicknesses.

Art Clay® Silver 650
This formula requires the lowest firing temperature of the Art Clay line. Can be fired with glass, ceramics, selected gemstones, and sterling-silver findings. Comparable to PMC3.

Art Clay® Silver Paper Type
Comparable to PMC Sheet, although the Art Clay version is slightly larger and thicker. Similarities include that it:
• remains flexible and does not dry out
• can be folded
• can be cut with scissors or paper punches
• must be fired from a cold kiln in a programmable electric kiln.

Art Clay® Slow Dry
This formula contains a different binder and does not dry out as quickly, so:
• weaving, braiding, and molding can be more easily done
• clay must still be completely dry before firing
• pieces must be kept 3mm thick or less to ensure proper drying.

Art Clay® Low-Fire Silver Overlay Paste
This soft slip-type formula is water based and easy to use. With it you can:
• paint designs directly onto glazed porcelain, glass, or bisque
• bond other metal clays onto porcelain, glass, or ceramics.

METAL CLAY FIRING CHART

Type of clay	Attributes	Firing temperature	Firing time (minutes)	Shrinkage (percent)	Firing method
Art Clay® Silver 650 also known as ACS650	Strong formula, suitable for items which encounter stress. Can be fired with glass, ceramics, select gems, Cubic Zirconia, and sterling silver.	1435°F/780°C 1380°F/750°C 1290°F/700°C 1200°F/650°C	5 10 15 30	8-9	Hot Pot kiln/ butane torch/ programmable electric kiln
Art Clay® Silver - Overlay Silver Paste also known as Lowfire Silver Overlay Paste	Formulated to bond to high-fire porcelain glazes. Paint paste onto glazed porcelain, ceramics, or glass in thin layers. Use for repairing low-temperature fired pieces.	1435°F/780°C 1380°F/750°C 1290°F/700°C 1200°F/650°C	5 10 15 30	8-9	Butane torch/ programmable electric kiln
Art Clay® Silver 650/1200 Low-Fire	The moisturizing binder keeps clay from drying and allows for special techniques like braiding and weaving. Dry completely before firing.	1200°F/650°C	Fire from cold kiln 30	8-9	Butane torch/ programmable electric kiln
Art Clay® Gold 22K	Can be applied as a paste onto greenware metal clay.	1832°F/1000°C	60	15	Butane torch (paste), programmable electric kiln
Art Clay® Silver - Paper Type	Thin, flexible sheet which can be folded, cut, draped, or layered. Will not dry out. Difficult to repair before firing. Thicker than PMC Sheet®.	1562°F/850°C 1472°F/800°C	Fire from cold kiln 20 30	8-9	Programmable electric kiln
Art Clay® Regular Slow Dry	Takes five times longer to dry and has more elastic properties. Dry completely before firing.	1562°F/850°C 1472°F/800°C	Fire from cold kiln 20 30	8-9	Butane torch/ programmable electric kiln
PMC3®	Strong formula, suitable for items which encounter stress. Can be fired with glass, ceramics, select gems, cubic zirconia, and sterling silver.	1290°F/700°C* 1200°F/650°C* 1110°F/600°C*	10 20 45	10-12	Hot Pot kiln/ butane torch/ programmable electric kiln
Aura 22® (22K gold)	Creamy paste which can be painted onto fine silver. Works best on clean, just-fired, unburnished metal clay.	1562°F/850°C 1472°F/800°C	10 30		Butane torch/ programmable electric kiln
PMC Sheet® also known as PMC Paper	Thin, flexible sheet which can be folded, cut, draped, or layered. Will not dry out. Difficult to repair before firing. Fired sheet is flexible and a single layer can be easily cut or punched.	1650°F/900°C* 1560°F/850°C* 1472°F/800°C*	Fire from cold kiln 10 20 30	10-15	Programmable electric kiln
PMC+®	Suitable for items which encounter stress. Can be fired with Cubic Zirconia.	1650°F/900°C* 1560°F/850°C* 1472°F/800°C*	10 20 30	10-15	Programmable electric kiln
PMC® also known as PMC Standard	Use for items which do not encounter stress.	1650°F/900°C*	2 hours	25-30	Programmable electric kiln
PMC Gold® 24K	Alone, soft and unsuitable for items which encounter stress. Can be thinned to a paste and applied to fired silver clay.	1830°F/1000°C	2 hours	25-30	Butane torch (paste) programmable electric kiln

* For strongest results, fire at 1650°F/900°C for two hours.

AIDA CHEMICALS

MITSUBISHI MATERIALS

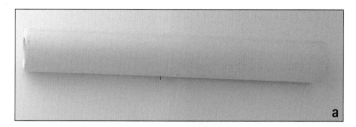

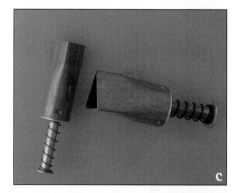

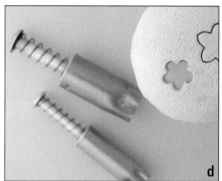

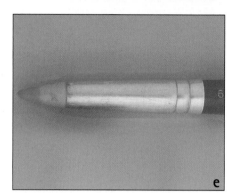

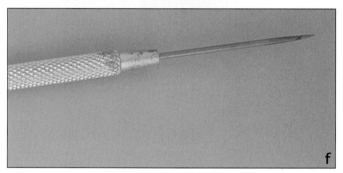

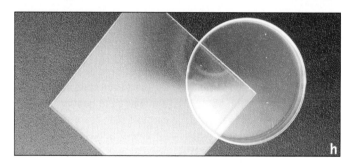

Tools for metal clay

Metal clay requires simple tools, many of which you may already have. Working with metal clay is easy to fit into almost any lifestyle—it takes up little space and both setup and cleanup are easy. Most of these tools could fit into a large Tupperware container. Start with these items and you can add others as you go along.

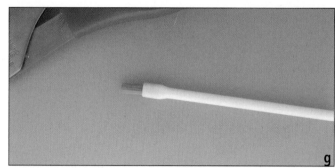

For wet metal clay:

Roller[a]
Cut a one foot length of ¾-in. diameter PVC pipe or purchase a small plastic or acrylic roller at the craft store. Oil the roller lightly so the clay will not stick.

Heavy plastic wrap
Cover your metal clay with heavy plastic wrap whenever you are not working with it to keep it from drying out.

Cutting tools [b]
An X-acto knife or craft knife is great for general shaping. Another useful cutting tool is a tissue blade, which looks like a long razor blade. The edge of a laminated playing card can also cut thinner pieces of clay.

Small pattern cutters [c-d]
are available at craft and cooking stores. Plain cookie cutters also work well, but these cutters have a spring mechanism to help remove the cut pieces.

Rubber-tipped clay shaper
[e] Quick-drying metal-clay slip tends to clump on paint brushes, so use a rubber-tipped shaper for applying it instead. The solid rubber is much easier to use and clean than a brush. Art supply stores usually carry a wide variety of different shapes and sizes.

Needle tool [f]
Use a needle tool or a round toothpick for defining lines and creating additional details.

Small brushes [g]
Small plastic makeup brushes are useful for smoothing dried metal clay.

Plexiglas® [h]
A small Plexiglas square or a clear, flat plastic lid is handy for rolling "snakes" or tiny, decorative balls.

Plastic straws
Drinking straws or small round, hollow cocktail straws cut clay circles with ease. They are also useful when forming cylinders of clay.

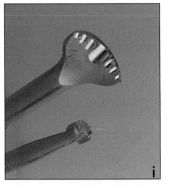

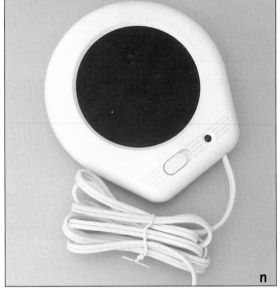

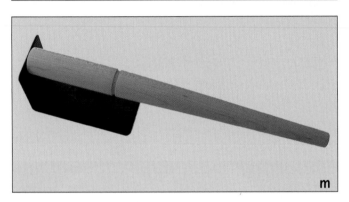

Texturing tools [i]
Leather-stamping tools and rubber stamps are fun to use and offer a wide range of textures that would otherwise be difficult to achieve. Fabric or lace can also be used to create texture.

Olive oil
Use small amounts of olive oil on your hands, tools, and work surface to prevent metal clay from sticking, and reapply it as needed while you work. The moment the clay starts to stick, it is time to add more. Olive oil will burn away with the firing. Other organic creams such as Badger Balm® are also good.

Playing cards or mat boards
To make even thicknesses of the clay, good quality playing cards or mat board cut into a frame shape is useful. Cards also come in handy to carry clay pieces and make stencils.

Non-stick work surface
Sheet protectors, flexible Teflon® baking sheets, plastic mats, glass countertop cutting boards, or sheets of styrene make good work surfaces. Coat the work surface with olive oil or hand balm. Flexible or movable surfaces enable you to move pieces of clay or easily pick up scraps. Avoid any type of aluminum tool or work surface, which can react negatively with the clay.

Cutting board
Use a cutting board to protect your work surface when cutting clay. Any plastic cutting board will work, but a flexible plastic or disposable cutting sheet is easy to store and convenient for travelling.

Airtight storage containers
[j] Film canisters or pill bottles with lids are perfect for storing metal-clay scraps and particles or for mixing and storing slip.

Spray bottle [k]
A small plastic spray bottle works well for misting clay to keep it moist. A jar of water enables you to moisten your fingers to join pieces or smooth seams.

Tweezers [l]
Tweezers are especially helpful when placing cubic zirconia (CZ) or other small objects in your design.

Ring mandrel [m]
Use a mandrel for sizing and shaping ring projects. Use a wooden ring mandrel which will not heat up during drying.

Drying tools [n]
A convenient tool for drying metal-clay pieces is a coffee cup warmer. Other tools you can use to speed up drying include a hair dryer, dedicated (to metal clay use) low-temperature toaster oven, or dedicated food dehydrator.

Metal Clay Magic

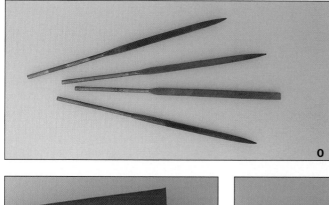

o

p

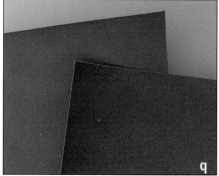

q

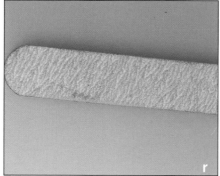

r

s

t

For dry metal clay:

Needle files [o]
Needle files are useful for getting into holes and finishing small spaces. These mini files are available online, through speciality hobby stores, or in jewelry supply stores.

Carving tools [p]
Wood carving tools or rubber stamp carving tools with a V-shape end work well on dried metal clay.

Sanding tools [q–s]
A variety of tools are available for sanding dried, unfired metal clay. For flat surfaces, 400- to 600-grit Wet/Dry sandpapers [q], which are available in hardware stores, work great. Sandpaper grit is determined by the number of abrasive particles per square inch, so the higher the number, the finer the grit. Start with the rougher grit. Good quality emery boards [r] are handy for sanding flat or curved surfaces. 3M produces sanding pads and a range of fine sanding/polishing papers up to 8000-grit [s]. These can be used for final sanding before firing or for polishing after firing.

Brushes [t]
Makeup brushes work well for many metal clay projects. Use small brushes for applying water or slip and large brushes for cleaning pieces after sanding. A very small, thin brush should be dedicated for using with gold clay. Small artist's paint brushes also work well to moisten joints or apply slip.

finding supplies

Cubic zirconia (CZ), X-acto knives, mandrels, needle tools, burnishing tools, polishing cloths, and liver of sulfur can be found at jewelry supply stores or online. Many other tools, such as cutting sheets, spray bottles, sanding papers, and butane torches are available from local hardware stores. Check office supply stores for plastic sheet protectors. Visit a local bead shop to find roundnose pliers, head pins, findings, and bails, and beads. Bead shops are also a great place to learn basic jewelry-making skills if you're new to the hobby.

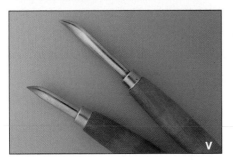

u

w

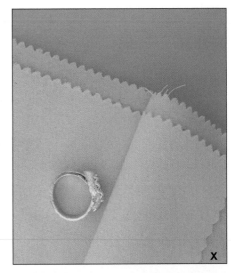

x

v

After firing:

Burnishing brush [u]

During firing, metal clay acquires an opaque white color. Use a soft brass brush to burnish the surface, which turns the white color into a satin finish. Most stainless steel or brass brushes work, but stiffer brushes will scratch the surface. Burnishing brushes are available through jewelry supply stores.

Hand burnisher [v]

To bring out a high shine, use a hand burnisher. This tool is especially useful when using the Keum-Boo technique to apply gold to metal clay.

Electric tumbler [w]

Use an electric tumbler when burnishing multiple pieces or to burnish faster. An electric tumbler requires stainless-steel shot and burnishing compound for silver and gold.

y

Polishing cloth [x]

These soft cloths are embedded with a polishing compound. Usually there are two pieces—one cloth for polishing and another for finishing. Jewelry stores often carry them, though they can sometimes be found in craft and beading stores.

Silver polish [y]

Cream-type polishes remove excess patina and bring out a nice shine.

Glue

Use E6000, an industrial strength, multipurpose glue, to connect pieces of clean, fired and burnished metal clay. Available at craft, jewelry supply, and hardware stores.

Beginner firing tools

Several options for firing metal clay exist. Some are quite inexpensive and easy to use while others require a greater investment of both time and money. The firing tools shown here are introduced in order from basic to more advanced equipment. Use the one which suits your needs and budget. See Chapter 2, "Tips and techniques," for more information on how to use the equipment, and be sure to read the manufacturer's instructions carefully. All the clays have different firing options. The chart on p. 10 gives you more information for each type of clay.

Hot Pot kiln [a]

Used extensively by metal clay enthusiasts in Japan, the Hot Pot kiln is portable, inexpensive, efficient, and very easy to use. The Hot Pot kiln comes packaged with 4 oz of fuel, which is enough for three firings. Fuel refills can be purchased. Each firing burns approximately 1.1 oz (about $1 worth) of fuel.

Though compact, the Hot Pot kiln can fire several small

a

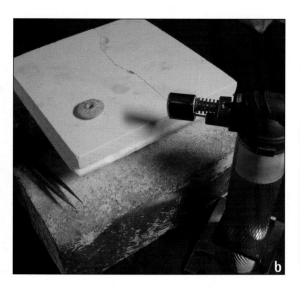

metal-clay pieces in just 15 minutes! Do not fire pieces heavier than 20g or larger than a half dollar. You can repeat the firing to ensure complete sintering.

Two versions of the Hot Pot are available—ceramic (as pictured here) and fiber. The fiber kiln may not break like the ceramic when dropped but it is also more expensive. The ceramic model costs less than $50. Hot Pot kilns are available through certified teachers or online suppliers. See "Resources and suppliers," p. 125.

Butane torch [b]

This is the same torch used to make crème brûlée. It is available in most hardware stores from about $30 to more than $60. Small pieces (less than 25 grams) made with PMC3 and Art Clay Silver 650 can be fired with a butane torch. It's particularly useful for gold work and is not as difficult as may be expected. Read about using a butane torch in Chapter 2, "Tips and techniques," before using.

Programmable electric kilns [c]

A programmable electric kiln is a necessity for some metal clay applications. If you need to fire a number of pieces simultaneously, include elements like glass, ceramics, sterling silver, or gemstones, or if you use PMC Sheet or Art Clay Silver Paper, you'll need a programmable electric kiln, which is the only firing tool that can accurately hold the necessary temperatures for the required amount of time. Your choice should have ramping capability (slowing down the heating or cooling) during firing. You should test your kiln, as it may have slight variations in temperature, especially if it is large. Electric kilns are the most expensive equipment used for metal clay work and can cost more than $500.

Sierra kiln (photo c, white kiln)

The Sierra kiln features a venting hole in the front. Some people think it's a peep hole, but do not look through it—you can damage your eyes by looking into hot kilns. The Sierra will hold the temperature within 4 to 8 degrees of your desired temperature. It has three pre-set programs and one user-defined program:
• PMC+ Fast = Full ramp, 1650°F, hold for ten minutes.
• PMC+ Slow = 1500 ramp, 1470°F, hold for 30 minutes.
• PMC Standard = Full ramp, 1650°F, hold for two hours.
• The user-defined program allows you to set your own program with up to four rates, temperatures, and hold times.

Though these programs carry the PMC name, they can all be used with either Art Clay or PMC products.

Paragon Rio kiln (photo c, blue kiln)

The Paragon Rio has a vent hole in the top with a plug to close the hole when desired. The vent hole is good for releasing smoke when using cork clay. Like the Sierra, it maintains temperatures within 4 to 8 degrees of the set temperature. It has five pre-set programs and one user-defined program:
• Pro 1—PMC+ Fast = Full Ramp, 1650°F, hold for ten minutes
• Pro 2—PMC+ Slow = 1500 ramp, 1470°F, hold for 30 minutes.
• Pro 3—PMC3 Slow = 1500 ramp, 1110°F, hold for 30 minutes.
• Pro 4—PMC Standard = Full ramp, 1650°F, hold for two hours.
• Pro 5—PMC Gold = Full ramp, 1830°F, hold for two hours.
• The user-defined program allows you to set your own program with up to eight ramps and temperatures. You can use this program for annealing and flask burnouts for casting.

Other programmable kilns

Art Clay World recommends the SC series kilns from Paragon Industries. The SC-2 is the same as the Rio Kiln and is the most popular kiln for firing Art Clay, while the SC-3 is essentially a larger version. Art Clay World also recommends and sells the multipurpose Caldera Kiln, a kiln with similar controls and different features. This kiln has a higher temperature range, and is top-loading and easy to repair.

These kilns can be used for tasks other than firing metal clay, including enameling, fusing glass, and annealing lamp work beads. Each kiln has its fans and critics. For more information, visit the web sites listed in "Resources and suppliers," p. 125. If you do not wish to own an electric kiln but want to try high-temperature metal clays, ask local certified teachers to fire your pieces. Many will fire metal clay for a small fee.

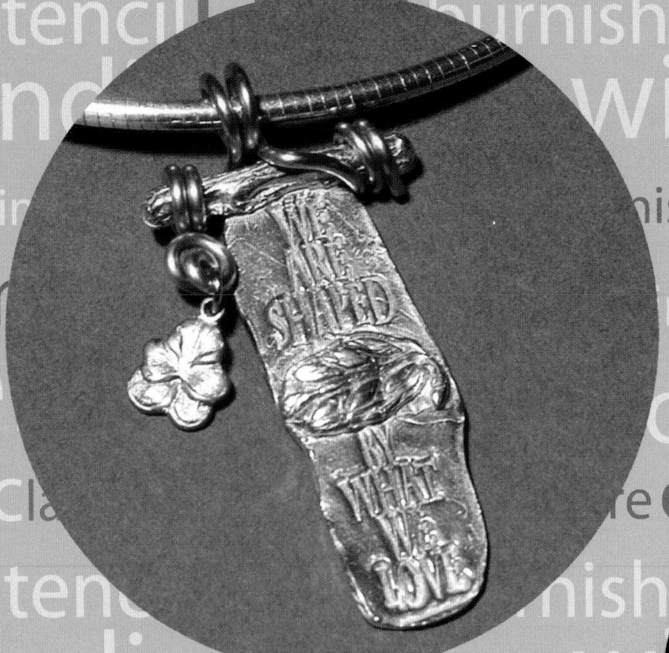
WE ARE SHAPED BY WHAT WE LOVE

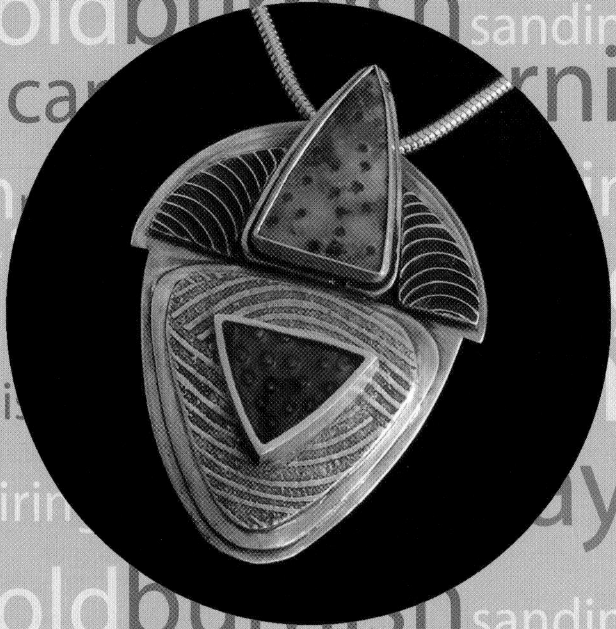

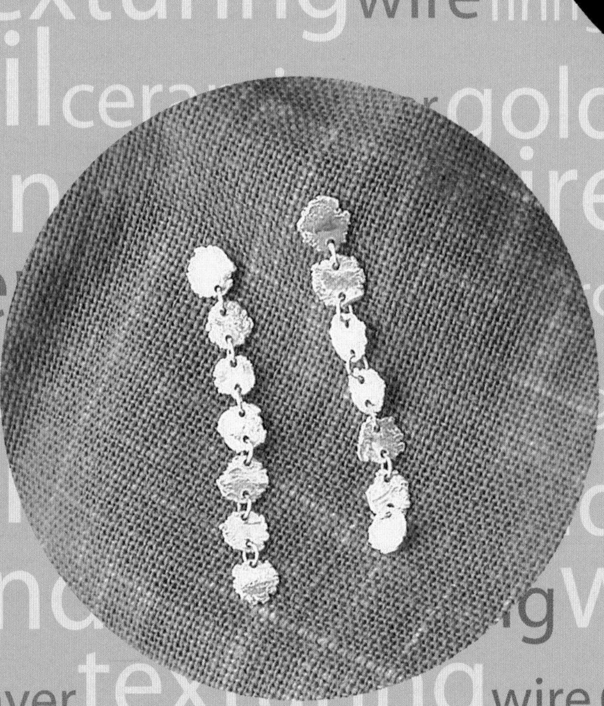

Tips and techniques

Metal clay artists have borrowed techniques from several artistic disciplines, including pottery, metalsmithing, scrapbooking, and others. Metal clay can be stamped, textured, layered, carved, molded, folded, burnished, cut, and more. It can be combined with other media, like fine-silver wire, glass, and ceramics. So many approaches to working with metal clay exist that it's hard to imagine running out of new things to try. The following pages address a number of ways to work with metal clay—from what to do with the clay when you first get it, to shaping and finishing, to incorporating other materials.

Closckwise from upper left: Stamped pendant by Sally Evans, Andrea Flanagan photo; Pendant with petrified palmwood stone by Linda Warner, Linda Warner photo; Disc earrings by Anna M. Aoki, Nancy Larkin photo.

Keep your metal clay moist

Before you open the metal clay package, be prepared to keep the metal clay from drying out. In dry climates, like that of Colorado where I live, metal clay dries very quickly. But even in humid climates, you need to be prepared. When metal clay dries out, it cracks and becomes difficult to work. Read the following before opening your first metal clay packet.

Work with wet metal clay quickly

Gather all your materials and tools before you start working with the clay. Ideally, you want to spend the least amount of time manipulating the wet clay, the majority of the time refinishing the clay once it dries, and only a little more time firing and finishing your piece. Envision what you want the final piece to look like—decide what textures and elements you will use, and the order in which you'll fabricate the parts. Minimize the amount of time you work with the wet clay and if an element is not ready to dry, keep it covered with plastic wrap, occasionally mist it, and add extender. Don't worry about the edges and non-textured surfaces—you can work on those when the clay is leather-hard.

Feel and remember

The consistency of metal clay when you first take it out of the package is its ideal state. Unlike polymer clay, metal clay does not need to be kneaded or conditioned before use. Keep in mind that the longer you work with the clay, the more likely it is to dry out, so avoid handling wet clay too much.

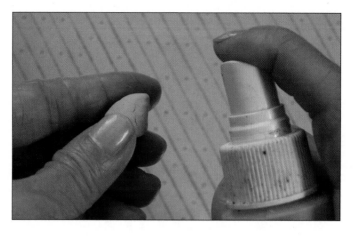

Keep water nearby

Have a small bowl of distilled water or a small spray bottle (see photo above) handy and, from time to time, add a few drops of water to your metal clay. Tap water is fine although it can sometimes cause mold to grow on the clay. The mold is not harmful to the clay and, since mold is organic and will burn away during firing, it is mainly a matter of aesthetics.

Use an extender

A trick I learned from Mary Ellin D'Agostino of the PMC Guild is to mix two parts glycerin with one part distilled water. Put this solution in a dropper bottle, then you can add a drop or two to the metal clay when needed. Other formulas which claim to keep metal clay from drying out have become available. See "Resources and suppliers," p. 125.

Use a thick organic hand cream

Before working with metal clay, wash your hands with warm water and then rub olive oil, Badger Balm, or another organic skin cream on your hands to keep the metal clay moist (and your hands soft!). The organic oils are non-toxic and will burn away during firing.

Use waterproof barriers

Work on a plastic sheet protector, plastic mat, or flexible plastic baking sheet that is lightly coated with oil—do not use paper, wood, or cloth. Whatever materials come in contact with your metal clay can absorb the moisture. Have a piece of heavy-duty plastic wrap ready to wrap around metal clay you are not working on. Keep flat metal-clay pieces from drying out by placing them inside a sheet protector or under layers of plastic wrap.

Store in airtight containers

Wrap unused metal clay that's been removed from its packaging in plastic wrap. Place it inside an airtight container along with a piece of wet paper towel to keep it hydrated.

Don't despair if it dries up!

If you find your metal clay has dried out, you can revive it by chopping it up with a food chopper that is dedicated to metal clay use. Then place the pieces in a film canister, add distilled water, and let it sit. If it is too wet to knead, pour it out on plastic wrap. Let it dry for a few minutes and then knead the metal clay with the plastic wrap—that way you can avoid getting your fingers messy as you work it back to the right consistency. If metal-clay particles stick to the plastic wrap, they will peel away easily when the clay dries.

Don't waste your metal clay

Although your first lump of metal clay may look very modest, you may be surprised at how much you can make by just being careful not to waste it. From a 25 gram packet, I can easily make 10 to 15 pairs of small, simple earrings. Metal clay is not inexpensive, so you will want to make the most of what you have.

Work on a plastic sheet protector
Use this flexible, non-stick surface to easily collect any stray pieces and slide them into airtight storage containers.

Collect unused clay
Any clay you trim off, or any clay left on the tools, work surface, straws, or your hands can be saved. If the metal clay is still moist, immediately wrap it in heavy-duty plastic wrap, tuck it back into the original metal clay package, and seal it.

Scraps and particles from sanding or carving which have dropped on the plastic sheet can also be saved. My favorite metal clay storage containers are plastic film canisters (see photo at left). Mark one container for scraps, the other for slip (see "Metal-clay slip," on p. 21). Spray distilled water in both containers periodically so that slip and scraps remain moist.

Rub your hands together to remove metal clay stuck on fingers. Let the metal clay on tools dry on the plastic sheet and you can peel or scrape it off later. Or keep handy a bowl of water in which you can wash off the metal clay. The metal clay will sink to the bottom. Drain away the water and scrape the soft metal clay into the slip container.

Avoid contamination
Be careful to not work where you use plastics or synthetic materials such as polymer clay. Particles of polymer clay will contaminate the metal clay and leave blemishes in the fired piece.

It's never too late!
Metal clay will not go bad, but, when reconstituted, will never be as smooth as it was fresh out of the package. If you dry your metal clay and decide you don't like it, chop it into small pieces and use it as slip. If you fire it and then decide you don't like it, either save it to refire with another piece (I have a box of odd fired pieces which might work with another piece in the future) or sell it to a silversmith or fine-metal recycler such as Rio Grande. Fired metal clay is .999 silver and can be treated as regular fine silver.

Rolling out a flat piece

Textured or smooth, rolled-out metal clay can be used for many projects. Achieving the right thickness is critical.

Preparing a surface
Use a plastic sheet protector with the seams cut so that it opens like a book. Rub a small amount of olive oil on the inside of the sheet to prevent the clay from sticking.

Selecting a rolling tool
A roller such as a small rolling pin, a polymer clay roller, or a clean 12-in. piece of ¾-in. diameter PVC pipe works well.

Shims
Use shims to roll metal clay to an even thickness. Shims can be made from playing cards, foam rubber sheets, or mat board strips [a]. If you use playing cards, stack them to the desired thickness and tape them together. Put the appropriate number card on top (so a stack three cards thick has a 3 on top). You will always use stacks in pairs, so make two of each thickness that you need.

Another way to make a shim is to cut out a "frame" from foam rubber sheets or mat board. The advantage of this method is that as long as the ends of the roller stay on the frame, you never worry about rolling off the end and causing uneven thicknesses.

Rolling out metal clay
Place the shim(s) inside the plastic sheet protector with the metal clay in the center. Clay should be rolled to a minimum thickness of three playing cards. Thinner than that, the clay becomes difficult to work with, especially when wet. If you are going to texturize the surface, start

with clay that is thicker— four or five cards thick— because the clay will become thinner as you texture it.

Put the cover of the plastic sheet back over the clay and cards [b]. This will prevent the clay from drying out.

Use a rolling tool to gently roll on top of the plastic sheet, squeezing the clay flat (the roller will not be in direct contact with the clay). Keep the roller ends on the shim to ensure that the clay maintains an even thickness [c].

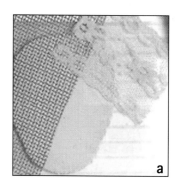

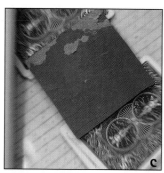

Texturing rolled-out flat pieces

Capture the delicate impressions of lace, leaves, mesh, and other flat, textured objects! First roll out a thick (about four or five playing cards thick), flat metal-clay piece. Leave the metal clay and cards inside the plastic sheet protector.

Making texture with a roller

Place the textured item directly on the metal clay [a]. Place the plastic cover back over the texture item, clay, and cards. Using one firm, smooth motion, roll the roller over the texture item. The clay will thin out as you texture it.

Using a rubber stamp

If you are using a rubber stamp, remove the hard backing. You will find it easier to peel metal clay from a flexible, flat rubber stamp than one with a hard-backing. Apply a thin coat of olive oil on the clean rubber stamp either by rubbing it on using your finger or by spraying the oil from a small spray bottle [b]. Roll out a piece of clay four cards thick. Place a stack of three cards on each side of the metal clay and position the edge of the stamp on top of the cards [c].

Use the roller to roll firmly once over the stamp.

Gently peel the rubber stamp off the metal clay (or peel the metal clay off the stamp) [d]. You should have a crisp impression on an even thickness of metal clay.

Other textures

You can use other textures on flat metal clay. Combs and plastic caps make good designs. In the Funky heart pin (p. 46), I used a toothpaste cap (here's another reason to save small objects rather than throw them out!). I simply rolled the toothpaste cap gently across the flat metal clay in a couple of different directions.

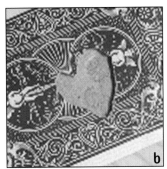

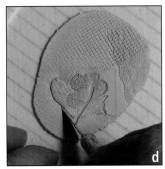

Stencils

A stencil is a handy way to cut out the right size and shape from a rolled flat metal-clay piece. A stencil also allows you to quickly make multiples of a shape. To make earrings, simply flip the stencil over to make a mirror image of the first one. You can also use the stencil lines in the design itself to create a border around a texture.

Making a stencil

Make a stencil by first drawing a few designs on a playing card [a]. Fine-point permanent markers work best on a card's shiny surface. Make the stencil a little larger than the desired finished size of the piece. Remember that the metal clay will shrink about 8-30% depending on the type of clay and that you will also sand it down. Select one drawing and cut the shape out [b]. You will use the card with the shape cut out of it, so don't worry about cutting into the center of the shape.

Using a stencil

Roll out a sheet of metal clay to a thickness of five cards. Cover the metal clay with the plastic sheet cover to keep the clay from drying out. Hold your stencil above the plastic sheet cover and decide what textured section to use. After you have decided on the section, lift the plastic sheet and place the stencil directly on the metal clay.

Using your fingers or a tool, gently press along the edges of the stencil so that an impression line remains on the metal clay [c].

Cut out the shape, going a little outside the line since you will be sanding down later on. You can also incorporate this line into the design [d].

Metal-clay slip

Slip is metal clay softened and thinned with water. It's useful for joining metal-clay pieces together and making repairs. Metal-clay slip or paste is available for purchase (see "Resources and suppliers," p. 125), but I like to make my own by recycling the scraps and sandings from earlier projects. Always keep different types of clay separate.

Making slip

When you sand metal clay, retain the clay dust in a container, add a few drops of distilled water, and gently mix them together. Let the slip sit, then add more water gradually. The slip should be a smooth, creamy consistency without lumps. It does take time for the metal clay to soak up the water, especially if you are using large scraps, so prepare the slip at least a few hours before you need it.

Water and tools

Avoid tap water, as it often causes an unsightly mold to grow on the clay. This mold will actually burn away during firing, but it looks unattractive. Use a small plastic makeup spatula to mix the slip.

Avoiding air bubbles

Avoid vigorous stirring or whipping the slip—it may create air bubbles which cause blisters in the fired clay. If you see bubbles in the slip, tap the slip container gently to get the bubbles to rise to the surface and wait until they burst or use a pin to break them.

Have slip ready

You should always have more than one slip jar—one that contains slip that is ready to use and another containing larger scraps that are soaking up water and softening.

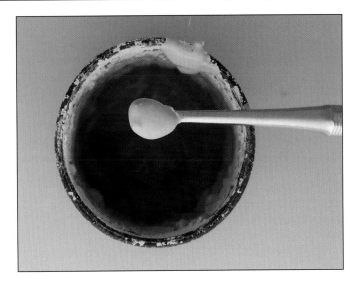

Finding the right consistency

Thin slip should be about the consistency of body lotion while thick slip can be like mayonnaise or face cream. It should be sticky enough to hold dried metal-clay pieces together.

Using slip

Use a small makeup brush or a paint brush when applying thin slip. Keep the brush in a cup of water when you aren't using it to keep the end soft. As the slip dries, it shrinks, so you may have to add several coats to fill holes and gaps.

To apply a generous amount of the thick slip, use a rubber-tipped clay shaper tool. Small strokes will help you avoid creating air pockets. If you apply too much slip, you can sand off any excess after it has dried.

Layering

Layering different textures and shapes creates depth and interest. Whenever you add a smaller top layer to a bottom layer, it is best to texture, cut, dry, and sand the pieces separately. This way, you can avoid distorting the textures on each piece and you can also sand and trim each piece separately so that all the lines and edges are neat and clean. **Photo a** shows an example of a layered pendant.

Preparing the pieces
Roll out and texture flat pieces or make a molded form for the top layer (see "Making a mold," p. 28). Cut out a background or bottom textured piece, a top flat textured or molded piece, and, if desired, a bail. Dry and sand each piece separately.

Attaching a top layer
When adding top layers or appliquéing, avoid trapping air by applying a thick glob of slip to the middle of the pieces to be joined together, rather than along the edges.

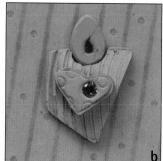

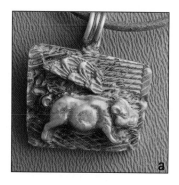

Press the two pieces together so that they stick. Dry completely before firing.

Attaching a bail [b]
Place the background piece facedown on a playing card.

Apply thick slip where the bail and background piece will join. Apply a generous amount of thick slip over the seam on the back side to ensure a strong bond. Dry, and sand smooth.

The sandwich method

This is just one method for making small hollow forms without using a core. This method involves layering three flat pieces together and connecting them with slip. One piece will be the top, one will be the middle layer, and the other will be the bottom.

Making the sides
Start by making a stencil in the shape you want [a]. A symmetrical shape is easiest to start with. Use the stencil to cut out three pieces from a thick, textured flat piece of metal clay. If the design is not symmetrical, reverse the stencil so that the opposite sides will both have the textured side facing out.

Select the worst-looking piece to become the middle layer and slice it in half. Place all four pieces on a small support, like a playing card [b]. Allow them to dry thoroughly.

Gently carve out the edges on one side of each of the middle pieces [c], so that there will be an open space

in the middle when the three layers are placed together. You should have four pieces—the top, the bottom and the two carved-out middle pieces [d].

Assembling the sandwich
Try layering all the pieces to see if they fit. The textured sides should be facing out. Do not worry if the edges are rough at this point—you will sand them down later. Now, using a generous amount of thick metal-clay slip, stack the pieces [e–f], making sure to put the two hollowed-out sections facing each other in the middle. Place the form back on the support and let it dry completely.

Sanding the outside
The sandwich piece will be very rough around the middle. Sand all around the middle layer to a smooth finish using sandpaper, going from a coarse grit to the finer 600 grit [g]. Use a round sanding tool or a small piece of sanding paper to smooth out a hole if you are making a bead [h].

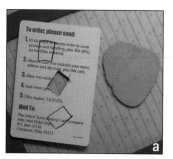

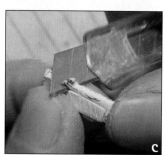

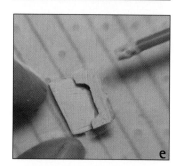

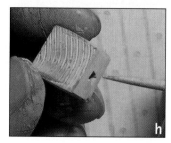

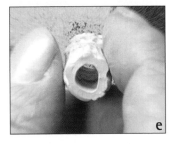

Creating a cylinder

The key to creating a good cylinder is to work quickly. Have a short straw or other cylindrical form oiled and ready to wrap the moist clay around.

Making a cylinder or tube
Roll out and, if you want, texture the metal clay. Quickly roll the moist metal-clay piece around the straw, overlapping the edges [a].

Use a card or craft knife to cut through the overlapping edges [b]. Remove the scraps and gently press the seam just enough to hold it together.

Now decide how wide the cylinder will be. Use a rolling motion as you cut around the straw to slice through the clay at the desired width [c].

Let the clay dry just long enough on the straw so it holds its shape [d]. Gently slide the cylinder off the straw, and let it dry thoroughly. If you can, apply more silver clay to the inside of the seam to stabilize the form. Dry again.

Holding the cylinder gently with three fingers, sand the edges on a flat surface that is covered with 400-grit sandpaper. Use a circular motion so the entire edge gets sanded evenly [e–f].

Making a closed-end cylinder
If you wish to make this a closed-end tube, cut out circular pieces a little larger than the diameter of the cylinder. Let the clay dry to a leather-hard state. Then use a small brush to apply a little slip to one end of the tube and place the circle over the opening.

Dry again and sand down the edges.

Drill a small hole in an end of the cylinder by gently twisting a jeweler's file or the point of a craft knife. It is not safe to fire a metal-clay piece without at least one small hole in it as otherwise it will explode when it is fired.

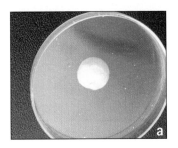
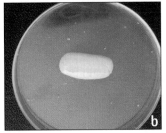
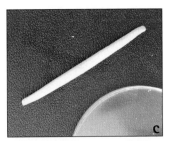
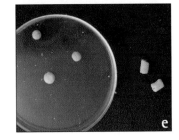

Rolling snakes

Snakes can be used to create smooth, even bands for ring projects, tapered pieces, swirls for pendants or brooches, or tiny silver balls.

Making the snake
Use a small clean sheet of Plexiglas® or a flat plastic lid with a bit of olive oil rubbed on the surface. Place a pea-sized piece of clay in the center [a]. Start gently rolling the metal clay with a side to side motion so that a smooth "snake" begins to form [b].

Keep moving from side to side so that the snake is solid, smooth, and of even thickness.

Making shapes
Make a tapered piece by applying more pressure to one end while rolling [c]. Before the clay begins to dry, shape the snake into a band, swirl, or other shape, or cut it into equal-sized pieces for tiny balls [d].

To make tiny balls, place several pieces of clay under the plastic lid. Cover the rest to prevent them from drying out. Using a gentle circular motion, roll the small pieces into tiny balls that are all of equal size [e].

Place the balls in a small tray or a small bowl to prevent them from rolling away while you make more. Dry the balls completely.

Attaching the shapes
With metal-clay slip and tweezers, attach the balls to the jewelry piece. Let dry completely [f]. Gently sand, if needed.

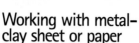

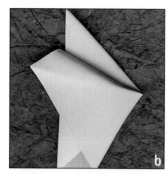

Working with metal-clay sheet or paper

Metal-clay sheet or paper [a] is available in two brands: Art Clay Silver Paper Type and PMC+ Sheet, also known as PMC Paper. Metal-clay paper is very different from regular metal clay in that it is very flexible and will not dry out.

You can work with metal-clay paper in almost the same way that you can work with thick paper. It can be folded [b], cut, trimmed, and even written on. (See "Message jewelry," p. 88.) You can cut metal-clay paper with scissors, paper cutters, paper punches, pinking shears, or even tear it with your hands. It can also be lightly textured. But unlike regular metal clay, it cannot be "repaired" once it is cut.

For now, metal-clay sheets only come in the higher firing-temperature formula. This requires the use of a programmable electric kiln.

Avoiding water

Water, which will cause metal-clay paper to disintegrate, should be avoided or used very sparingly unless you are deliberately trying to "melt" the paper. For this reason I suggest firing metal-clay paper separately before attaching it to other metal-clay forms or applying metal-clay slip. Keep your hands and tools dry.

Uses of metal-clay paper

Metal-clay paper was originally made for making origami (folded paper) pieces [c], but try other techniques. It can be textured, sliced into strips and woven, cut into delicate shapes [d] and layered onto other metal-clay pieces, or draped to resemble cloth.

Firing metal-clay paper

Because metal-clay paper is thin, it needs to be supported to hold its shape until after firing. By itself, a single layer of metal-clay paper will bend and tear.

Metal-clay paper will not dry out, but keep any unused metal-clay paper wrapped in plastic to keep it from oxidizing and turning brown.

Texturing metal-clay sheets

You can use leaves and other flat objects to texture metal-clay sheets. Place the metal-clay sheet inside a flat cellophane bag or a plastic sheet protector. Place the textured object directly on top of the metal-clay sheet. Use a hard burnishing tool or metal spoon and rub firmly on top of the plastic [e].

Typing on metal-clay sheets

Type messages directly onto a metal-clay sheet with a typewriter [f]. Tape an entire piece of metal-clay sheet onto a letter-sized sheet of paper, just barely covering the four edges of the metal-clay sheet. Open up the paper release on the typewriter and slide the paper with the metal clay into position. Close the paper release to hold the metal-clay sheet in place. Type words or phrases over the entire sheet [g]. Cut the metal-clay sheet into the desired sizes and shapes.

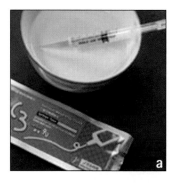

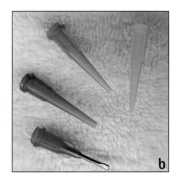

Using metal-clay syringe

Have water handy

When using the syringe, it's good to have a bowl of water handy. When you are not using the syringe, keep it tip-down in the water [a] to keep the metal clay in the tip from drying out. If there is extruded clay to discard or clay stuck on tools or fingers, gently wipe it off in the bowl of water. The metal clay will sink to the bottom of the bowl. Later, you can drain off the water and recover the metal clay to re-use as slip.

Syringe tips

The syringe comes with one tip which you can modify by cutting it. For a very thick coil, use no tip. You can purchase a syringe tip set [b] separately for a variety of forms (see "Resources and suppliers," p. 125).

Practicing with the syringe

Practice on your plastic sheet cover or on a fired metal-clay sheet [c]. The trick is to keep a steady hand while pressing on the syringe. I use one hand to squeeze and the other to provide support to the hand pressing the syringe.

Allowing for shrinkage

When applying the syringe clay to a fired piece, remember that as the metal clay is fired, it will shrink and pull on the fired piece, causing it to buckle. To alleviate shrinkage, apply the metal-clay syringe in small curves ("frosting-style") so that it can give as it shrinks. If you extrude a line that is not to your liking, simply remove the clay with tweezers or a toothpick once it has dried. Drop the extruded clay into a bowl of water or your slip container.

Creating a raised design

Use syringe-type clay to create a wonderful raised design like the one in **photo d**. Use no tip and apply the metal clay to a dried but unfired metal-clay slab. With a damp makeup brush, draw lines where the extruded clay will go. Apply the syringe clay to the piece. Gently press the extruded clay to ensure that there are no gaps. Dry the piece completely, and then gently sand the extruded clay against a piece of sandpaper laid flat on the table. After firing, use a brass brush to burnish the entire piece to a soft satin finish. Then use a hard burnishing tool on just the raised design for a high shine.

Hollow forms

A number of ways to make hollow metal-clay pieces exist, four of which are covered in the following two pages. No matter which method is used, be sure to keep these guidelines in mind:

• Have at least one hole for the hot, expanding air to escape from while the metal clay is firing.

• Keep the walls of the hollow form consistent—avoid thin spots next to thick spots. As the metal clay dries and is fired, it will shrink (see the chart on p. 10) but the thin areas may split open as the thicker areas pull harder.

Determining the thickness of the walls

The thickness of the walls is determined by the size and shape of the piece. A very small, simple piece will hold up with surprisingly thin walls while a larger, complicated piece will require thicker walls. Celie Fago has designed beautiful, textured small boxes and beads which require walls of only two- to three-card thicknesses.

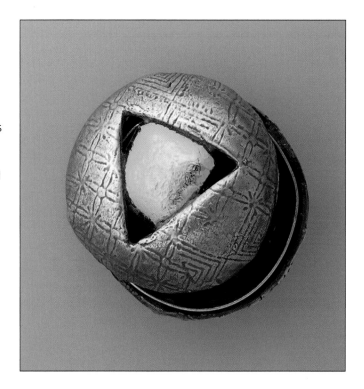

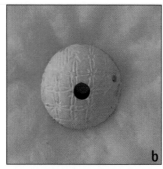

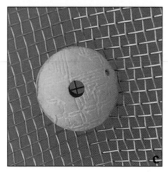

Support the piece

If the hollow piece is round or oddly shaped, fire it on supporting materials, such as vermiculite [a] or alumina hydrate in a small terra-cotta dish. A fiber blanket [b], also known as "refractory ceramic," or "doll prop" resembles cotton wool in appearance. This fiber blanket can also support metal-clay pieces. I prefer vermiculite since the particles are not too fine and it is readily available in garden stores. Vermiculite will eventually crumble with repeated firings, so replace it occasionally.

Be careful not to let the support materials fall inside the hollow form. As the piece fires and shrinks, anything inside will push against the walls, causing dents. CAUTION: Alumina hydrate is made up of fine particles that are harmful if inhaled. A respirator is recommended when using this material. The fiber blanket should also be handled with care. (See "Firing with electric kilns," p. 33, for more information.)

Firing hollow forms in a Hot Pot kiln

If you are using the Hot Pot kiln, shape a small piece of stainless-steel wire mesh [c] into a small rack to be the support for firing round shapes. Place this support on top of the circular mesh wire inside the Pot.

Using a core

Larger, oddly-shaped metal-clay pieces [d] may require a support core. This can be a soft, moldable material such as Cork Clay or florist foam, or other materials which will burn away during firing such as pasta [e–f], paper, cereal, or twigs.

You may need to apply a thin layer of low-melt beeswax or fabric glue to the core. This sticky layer will help the metal clay stick to the form and also allow room for the shrinkage of the metal clay. If the clay shrinks before the core has burned away, cracks or burst seams may result.

Textured layers of metal clay can be wrapped around the core and joined together by gently pressing the seams together with a rubber-tipped shaper tool. The clay can also be lightly textured after sheets are wrapped around the core. The pendant pictured here [d] was textured after the base layer was wrapped around the core.

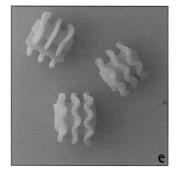

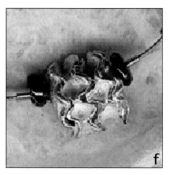

If you are applying metal-clay slip around a core, apply several layers, drying between each layer until it is about three playing cards thick. If the core is oddly shaped, such as a pasta piece, take care to apply thicker layers to both the crevices and ridges.

The metal clay should be three to five playing cards thick depending on how large the piece is. Whether or not you are using a core, the piece must be dried before firing. Fire the piece in a well-ventilated area. The core will produce smoke as it burns out. CAUTION: If the core material is not an organic, natural material, you need to take precautions to avoid inhaling toxic fumes.

Making a hollow, coreless form

One type of hollow, coreless form is known as a Lentil Bead. I learned of this method second-hand but I believe Celie Fago first used it for metal clay. Roll out a flat layer of clay and leave it smooth or texture it lightly. For smaller forms, use metal clay that is two to three cards thick; for larger forms, use thicker layers. To make one lentil bead, cut out two circular shapes. Place the two circular flat pieces on two smooth, oiled round objects. Ping pong balls, light bulbs, or round glass balls work well. Allow them to dry completely.

Sand the lips of the two pieces so that they join together snugly. Apply thick slip to the entire lip of one disk, then join the two together and dry. Here I carved out shapes on one side and painted gold metal clay inside the beads [g].

You can also create hollow forms by making cylinders or using the sandwich method (see "Creating a cylinder," p. 23, and "The sandwich method," p. 22).

The carve-out method

This method uses a mold, and works well if you are molding the metal clay into an unusual three-dimensional form. A mold can capture interesting shapes and textures such as those of shells [h], pine cones, pods, and other items. By partially drying the piece, you can keep the walls a consistent thickness (see "Making a mold," p. 28).

After firmly pressing a generous amount of metal clay into the mold, pop the clay out of the mold, and texture it as desired. Place the molded metal clay on a plastic support or a small ceramic dish with the flat side down and the molded side facing up. Dry the piece, with the textured side up, in a warm oven for about 5 minutes. Test the piece by touching the surface. The molded and textured surface should be dry and hard, but the inside should still be soft and moist. Do not overdry! This method will keep the outside texture and shape from becoming distorted and you will be able to feel the drier clay as you carve out the inside of the piece, allowing you to keep the walls a consistent thickness.

Using a small carving tool and supporting the piece with three fingers, gently carve out the inside [i]. As you carve, you will feel the harder, drier metal clay on the outside surface. Stop carving when the outside is about 1/8 in. (4mm) thick. After carving out the two sides, join the parts together with metal-clay slip. Dry the piece.

Making origami forms

Another interesting version of a hollow form is the origami shape made using metal-clay paper. In this case [j], I made a balloon by gently blowing into a folded metal-clay sheet. This is a popular design often featured in origami books for children. The result is an interesting, lightweight, hollow bead.

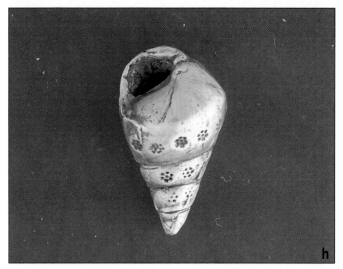

Making a mold

Two-part silicone molding compound
Although this material is expensive, I recommend it because it's very easy to use. Several brands are available: Belicone, PCE, and others. They work by combining two parts [a] which then harden within minutes into a durable, flexible mold. Almost any item can be molded: buttons, shells, pine cones, fingers— use your imagination! You can even make molds of your favorite metal-clay pieces.

Making the mold
Have the object to be molded ready when you begin mixing together two equal parts of the compounds [b]. Initially there will be streaks of the two compound colors. As soon as the color is smooth— usually within a minute— press the object firmly into the compound, no more than halfway, and let it sit for 30 minutes at room temperature or as directed in the manufacturer's directions [c].

After the compound has set, remove the object from the mold [d]. The mold is ready to be used. Simply press the metal clay into the mold and immediately pop it out by gently flexing the mold. This type of mold usually doesn't require any oil or lubricants.

Creating a three-dimensional form
A three-dimensional form can be made by creating two molds. After making the first mold of one side, place a piece of heavy duty plastic wrap between the mold and the original object [e]. Add fresh molding compound on top of the object and the plastic wrap [f]. Let sit for 30 minutes. When you separate the molds and remove the object, you should end up with two molds which fit into each other [g].

Working with fine-silver wire

Metal clay is fine silver—pure silver (.999 percent silver) without other metals mixed in. Many jewelry pieces are made with sterling silver (.925 percent silver), which is silver mixed with copper for strength. Fine silver can be fired with metal clay without any problems, while sterling silver will blacken or develop firescale (a dark stain) during firing.

Fine-silver wire can be used as a ring band, a bail, or a decorative element. It is less expensive than metal clay, and helps make silver jewelry work more economical.

Properties of fine-silver wire
Fine-silver wire is available in different thicknesses which are measured by gauge. The lower the gauge number, the thicker the wire. 18-gauge is thin enough to handle easily, but it needs to be bundled into three- or four-wire thicknesses to be strong enough for a ring band.

Fine-silver wire is sold fully annealed (also known as "dead soft"). It is slightly softer than sterling silver and you will be able to bend fine-silver wire with your hands. As you bend and handle it, the metal will harden and stiffen. This is called work hardening. Thicker wire (less than 18-gauge) will harden quickly, making it difficult to work with.

Similar materials
Fine-silver bezel wire and sheets can also be used with metal clay. Its characteristics are the same as the wire. It fires well with metal clay, but the smooth surface makes it difficult for the metal clay to grip, so it's necessary to score the surface of any fine-silver bezel wire that is to be attached to metal clay.

Tools for working with wire
Besides your hands, the most useful tools for handling silver wire are flat nose pliers, round nose pliers, and wire cutters [a]. After you have shaped the wire, use flat needle nose pliers to slightly flatten it. This will smooth the surface of the band and strengthen the wire.

Attaching fine-silver wire to metal clay
Because the surface of wire is very smooth, it may slip out of

a metal-clay piece even after firing. To avoid this problem, slightly bend, cut, or smash the ends of the wire so that it can grip the metal clay [b].

Cover the ends of the wire with a generous amount of metal-clay slip [c]. Let dry and sand off excess clay.

After firing, a patina can be applied to fine-silver wire as well as to the burnished metal clay, if desired, as shown on the bail of the leaf pendant in **photo d**.

Drying metal clay

Ideally, you should work quickly with wet clay—apply the texture and then let it dry. But during the dry stage you can take your time. Metal clay (with the exception of the sheet-type metal clay products—see "Working with metal-clay sheet or paper," p. 24) needs to be bone dry before firing. If moisture gets trapped in the metal clay, it may expand as it heats, creating unsightly blisters.

Air-drying
Air-drying is the best way to avoid distortion of your object. Just let it rest overnight at room temperature. To accelerate air-drying, set your pieces on a sunny windowsill.

Drying on a cup warmer or hot plate
Because metal clay shrinks as it is dried or fired, using a heat source like a cup warmer or hot plate will speed up the drying process but might cause some distortion if one side dries faster than the other. A little distortion on a flat piece will probably flatten out naturally if the piece is fired on a flat surface.

To avoid too much distortion, try placing the flat metal-clay piece between two playing cards taped gently together and flip the piece periodically.

Controlled drying
Carving and keeping walls a consistent thickness is easiest when the metal clay is only partially dried to a leather-hard stage. Drying from one side allows a texture to be preserved while the other side is carved.

Drying a hollow form
To dry a finished hollow form, warm in a toaster oven or air-dry thoroughly.

Test for dryness
Use a playing card to pick up and move the hot clay. Metal clay from the toaster oven or hot plate can be very hot—I've picked up a piece only to suddenly drop it when I realized how hot it was! Different colors or shades in the clay might indicate that the piece is not completely dry. Dry clay is lighter in color than wet clay. CeCe Wire showed me one trick for judging dryness: after it cools, try placing the piece against your cheek. If it feels clammy, it probably needs to dry longer. When you sand the piece, if it sticks or doesn't sand easily, it probably needs to dry more. You can't over-dry a piece before firing so, when in doubt, go ahead and let it dry longer.

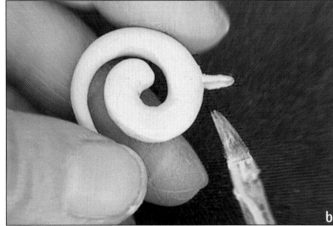

Carving and sanding metal clay

Some of the unique characteristics of metal clay are most apparent when the clay is dry but hasn't yet been fired. At this stage, when the clay is referred to as "leather-hard clay," you can employ a number of interesting techniques to obtain various finishes and results. It is much easier to smooth and shape the pre-fired metal-clay piece than to try to achieve the same results with the fired metal clay or finished silver work.

You can take all the time you need at this stage. Unlike the wet clay stage, you do not need to work fast to maintain the moisture. If you want to carve the metal clay, it is best to do that at the leather-hard stage where there is still some moisture in the metal clay. The leather-hard metal clay will feel cool and clammy when you place it against your cheek or the back of your hand. "Bone-dry" or "greenware" clay contains no moisture.

Carving

Carved metal clay has a natural and beautiful look. Carving metal clay is similar to carving wood. Dry the metal clay to the leather-hard stage. You can draw designs directly on the dried metal clay with a pencil, and then use woodcarving or rubber stamp carving tools to engrave the design.

You can also carve by setting the metal-clay piece on a nonslip surface such as a rubber block or a thick pad of paper. This way the piece can be turned as you work on it.

Practice carving so that the lines are smooth and neat shavings come off with each stroke.

Support the metal clay

Dry metal clay is very brittle, somewhat like chalk, so it needs to be firmly supported. But don't worry when you break your first piece—you need to experience firsthand how much pressure dried metal clay can withstand.

Repairing breaks

You can usually repair a simple break with metal-clay slip. If that doesn't work, recycle the pieces in your slip containers.

Sanding

Dry the metal clay to the bone-dry stage. Use standard wet/dry silicon sandpaper, available in hardware stores, in grit sizes from about 400 up to 600 [a].

Emery boards are an inexpensive, handy tool for sanding different shapes. Jeweler's needle files, available from metal clay suppliers, are useful for sanding tight corners or holes. Miniature needle sanding tools are wonderful for particularly small spaces (see Chapter 1, "Tools and materials").

To make flat surfaces perfectly smooth, lay a piece of sandpaper or an emery board on the work surface and, holding the metal clay perpendicular to the sanding material, move it in a circular motion. Do not press too hard or you may break the piece. You can also sand the ends of a cylinder or tube this way.

To achieve a smooth, mirror-like finish, use sandpaper or polishing paper in various grits. Begin with rougher grits, indicated by lower numbers, and work your way up to 1200 or higher.

As a final step, smooth over the surface with a damp brush or cosmetic sponge until all the cracks and bumps are gone [b].

Firing with the Hot Pot

The small, inexpensive Hot Pot kiln was introduced in Japan and is designed to fire low-fire metal clays such as PMC3 or Art Clay 650. It requires little space, fires quickly, and uses only about $1 worth of fuel with each firing. For most beginners, this is the kiln to start with.

Getting familiar with the Hot Pot kiln

The Hot Pot kiln [a] is composed of two sections (the bottom is larger and both sections of the pot are lined with a heatproof fiber blanket, which should not be removed), one round metal screen, two rectangular metal screens, a tile, fuel bottle (lasts about three firings), and a small terra-cotta pot. Use the Hot Pot in well-ventilated areas.

Preventing flare-ups

Bend one rectangular metal screen around the other rectangular screen, and then bend the two ends of the long piece down so that it is a "table" [b]. Place this "table" inside the top of the pot over the hole to prevent flames from shooting out [c].

Preparing the fuel pot

Place the small terra-cotta fuel pot inside the bottom portion of the Hot Pot and fill it to the top with fuel [d]. This pot may break after a few firings, but you can replace it with another small terra-cotta pot. If there are any holes in the bottom of the replacement pot, cover them with shards from the broken pot.

Placing the metal-clay piece

Put the round metal screen on the top of the bottom pot and place the metal-clay piece in the center. Avoid firing metal-clay pieces that are greater than 20g in total weight or larger than a half dollar. Keep the clay piece(s) in the center of the metal screen. Place the kiln on a stovetop with the fan on or in the garage. The fumes from the alcohol-based fuel can be irritating to the eyes and should be avoided.

Firing the Hot Pot kiln

Light the fuel through the hole on the side using a long-handled lighter [e]. You will hear a "poof" when it lights. With your metal-clay already in place, let it sit for 15 minutes. It will stop firing when the fuel runs out. Metal clay can be re-fired or fired longer with no problem.

In fact, a longer firing time will create stronger pieces.

Removing the piece

When firing is complete, be careful not to burn yourself. Use metal tongs to pick up the top of the kiln and the fired metal-clay piece. Let the piece cool before burnishing and polishing.

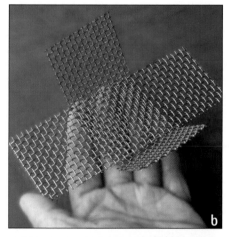

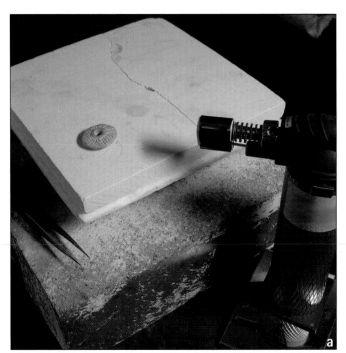

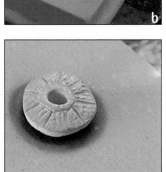

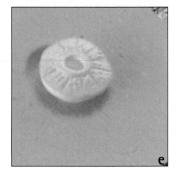

Firing with a butane torch

This is a good way to fire low temperature metal clays. Small pieces (less than 25 grams) made with PMC3 and Art Clay Silver 650 can be fired with a butane torch. Some of the other Art Clay® products can also be fired with a torch. See the chart on p. 10 for firing times and temperatures. Using a butane torch is not as hard as it looks, and besides, it is fun to actually watch the sintering process! Butane torches and fuel can be found at hardware or cooking supply stores. Torch prices range from about $30 to more than $60.

Setting the right temperature

Adjust the flame intensity to the appropriate heat level, if your torch is adjustable—many are not. Stay below the melting points of the metals (1760°F for silver, 1931°F for 22K gold) and over the minimum temperatures listed on the metal clay packets. A number of metal clay suppliers also sell torches that are calibrated to fire metal

clay at the right temperature. Be sure to check before you buy a torch so you get the features you want. In general, the less expensive torches have fewer features.

Preparing to fire

Prepare the work place and tools necessary for torch firing [a]. Have safety glasses, fine tweezers, and heavy leather gloves ready. Place two large bricks or soldering blocks on a metal tray. One brick will be the work surface. Place a ceramic-fiber tile (a small white tile which withstands high temperatures) on this brick. The other brick will hold a quenching bowl. CAUTION: Do not quench a piece that includes a CZ, glass, or lab-grown stone. They will shatter or crack if exposed too quickly to changes in temperature.

Turn the lights down. It will be easier to see the colors of the sintering piece without glaring lights. You will need a timer you can operate with one hand.

Learning the technique

With torch firing, you will rely on the color, surface appear-

ance, and size of the metal-clay piece to determine how long it should fire. Before you fire your first masterpiece, sacrifice a small piece of metal clay and over-fire it until the it has melted into a shapeless lump. Watch it carefully to recognize the different stages.

Be sure that the clay is bone dry. Any moisture in the clay might expand and cause the piece to burst. If you are torching a piece with a gemstone, be sure that it can withstand the heat. To prevent the stone from popping out, place it facedown.

Determining the firing time

Figure out the weight and size of the metal-clay piece to be fired and set the timer. A 20-25g piece will require a minimum of 3.5 to 4 minutes. A 15-20g piece, 3 minutes, a 10-15g piece, 2.5 minutes, and a 5-10g piece, 2 minutes. Under-firing will result in brittle clay. Firing longer will not harm the metal clay.

Firing the piece

Hold the torch at a 45-degree angle about 2 in. away from

the metal-clay piece [b]. Keep the flame moving, but always keep it on the metal-clay piece. You will see smoke and flames as the binders in the clay burn away [c]. Then the metal-clay piece will turn white and shrink [d], and a glow will appear, gradually turning to a warm reddish-orange [e]. If the glow turns into an intense orange or bright red, or the surface begins to shine, pull the torch back. The shine is the stage immediately before the silver melts completely.

When the clay reaches this ideal color, start the timer with your free hand. Keep the torch moving and watch the metal-clay piece carefully to avoid over-firing.

Once the timer goes off, you can let the piece air cool. If there are no gems or stones attached, you may pick up the piece with tweezers and quench it by dropping it into the quenching bowl. You can immediately remove the piece from the quenching bowl and begin the finishing steps or resume firing, if desired.

Firing with electric kilns

If you decide to invest in an electric kiln [a], be sure to consult "Resources and suppliers," p. 125, as well as the information on electric kilns in Chapter One.

The best electric kiln for firing metal clay is small and has programmable time and temperature controls. The firing temperature and time must be consistent, otherwise under- or over-fired pieces will result.

If you are planning to use glass, dichroic glass, or glass enamels with metal clay, the ramping feature (controlling the rate of heating or cooling) is handy.

Using the kiln

To maximize the space in your kiln, use kiln furniture [b], small blocks and tiles which can be stacked to make one, two, or three layers of shelf space. Since most metal-clay pieces are small, you can fire many pieces at once by using more shelves.

If the metal-clay pieces are of different shapes and require support, you will need a small terra-cotta dish or some type of heatproof container which can hold granular support material. Vermiculite, an organic gardening material made of mica, can be bought at any gardening store. Vermiculite is rather coarse and will break down with repeated firings, so it will need to be replaced from time to time. A fiber blanket can also be used. A fiber blanket resembles cotton or wool in appearance but it is a refractory ceramic fiber which can withstand the high heat of the kiln.

Note: Take care to not breathe the dust when handling any type of synthetic fiber material.

Guidelines for electric kilns designed for metal clay

Always read and follow the manufacturer's instructions. Set up the electric kiln at least 12 in. (30.5 cm) away from walls and furniture. Keep the space over the kiln open. The top of the kiln will get hot enough to burn your hand.

The bottom of the electric kiln is insulated and will not harm the surface the kiln is sitting on. But it is important to have a heatproof area nearby for the just-fired metal-clay pieces. I place a couple of bricks near the kiln. One brick will hold the quenching bowl, a heatproof bowl filled with water to cool the just-fired metal-clay pieces. Another brick will hold the hot tile from the kiln. Use heavy heatproof gloves and sturdy tongs to take the hot tile and metal-clay pieces out from the kiln. Do not touch the pieces until they are completely cool.

Ample electricity

The first time I used my electric kiln in my house, I blew the fuses! The electric kiln does use a lot of electricity—enough to make a noticeable increase in the electricity bill. To reduce the likelihood of blowing fuses, plug the kiln in where it will not be competing with other electrical appliances.

Place the kiln in a well-ventilated area. I have mine in front of the fireplace where I can conveniently vent it.

Metal clay and gemstones

Firing gemstones with metal clay

In some cases, you may want to include gemstones in a design. In order to withstand the heat of firing with metal clay, the gemstone needs to be stable enough to not shatter or discolor. Natural stones are often treated before they reach the consumer and this can affect how they might react in a kiln. If the gems are heat-treated, then they are not likely to change again when fired with a low-fire metal clay. But an irradiated gemstone or one which has inclusions may be damaged with firing.

Diamonds, quartz, amethyst, turquoise, and citrine are some of the gems which do not fire well. Garnet, hematite (shown here in this necklace by Arleen Alleman), and peridot are three of the few gems which are likely to survive firing with a low-fire metal clay. If you are unsure what the stone is or whether it will tolerate high heat, try firing the gem by itself first. Check the web sites in "Resources and suppliers," p. 125, for the latest on which gems are most likely to fire well with metal clay. Kevin Whitmore of Rio Grande has done extensive research and has posted a handy chart on natural gemstones at www.pmc-conference.com/techresources/seminars/gemstonechart.html.

Avoiding thermal shock

Heating or cooling too rapidly will crack many gems. You can sometimes avoid this by using an electric kiln which can be ramped 500°F per hour to a firing temperature of 1110°F and hold for 30 minutes. Cool slowly.

Using man-made gems

Man-made gems have the same chemical and optical properties as their natural counterparts but are purer and free of the small cracks and other elements found in natural stones. Most man-made gems are created at temperatures above that for firing metal clay (1650°F) and can be fired with low-fire metal clay. When purchasing such man-made gems, be sure to ask if they were created with high heat.

Adding gems after firing

Any gemstone can be added to a finished metal-clay piece. Use a ready-made fine-silver bezel cup, make a bezel using fine-silver ribbon, or make one yourself with metal clay. The ready-made fine-silver bezel cup can be fired with the metal clay. Insert the gem after burnishing and finishing. The fine-silver ribbon bezel will also not shrink but it might be safest to fire it with an already-fired metal-clay piece which is unlikely to shrink further. You need to factor in shrinkage if you are making a bezel out of metal clay for a particular stone (see "Shrinkage," p. 36).

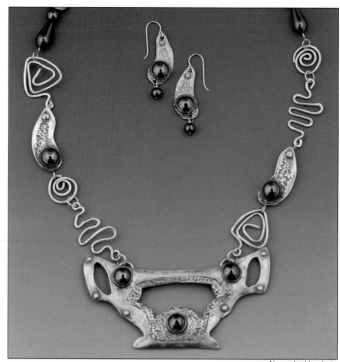

Nancy Larkin photo

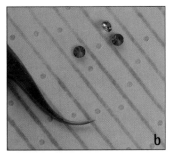

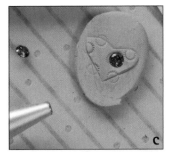

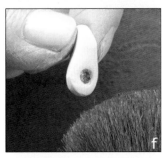

Firing with cubic zirconias (CZs)

Cubic zirconias (laboratory-grown stones often called CZs) come in a beautiful variety of colors and shapes. They add a wonderful sparkle to your silver creations [a] and are very easy to use!

Firing metal clay with CZs

Generally, CZs can be fired with metal clay, but check with your supplier to be sure the stones can withstand the firing temperature of the metal clay you've chosen.

Inserting the CZ

Use tweezers to handle the slippery little stones [b]. I like to use a retractable ball point pen with the end retracted as a tool to evenly press the CZ into the soft metal clay [c]. Simply set the CZ into the soft clay so that the widest part of the stone, the "girdle," is under the surface of the metal clay. As the metal clay fires, it will shrink around the CZ and grab the girdle.

Making a bezel

An easy way to make a simple bezel is to roll a small ball of metal clay slightly larger than the CZ. Just press the CZ into the metal-clay ball. After pressing the CZ stone into the metal clay, let the piece dry. Using a small, damp makeup brush, smooth the surfaces around the CZ stone and let dry again. **Photo d** shows a completed piece with a bezel made in this manner.

Preparing the CZ for firing

With a wooden toothpick, remove any metal clay from the surface of the CZ gem [e]. As a final step before firing, use a soft makeup brush to remove any remaining particles [f]. After firing, let the piece with CZ cool in the kiln. Sudden cooling by quenching in water will crack the CZ. **Photo g** shows an origami star highlighted by a bezel-set CZ.

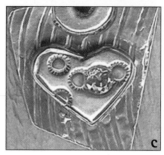

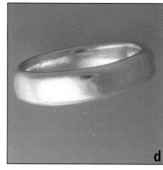

Shrinkage

Shrinkage [a] was a major
factor in the original form of
metal clay, which shrank 28
percent during the two-hour
firing time. PMC® Gold shrinks
25 to 30 percent and Art
Clay® Gold shrinks 15 percent.
Shrinkage has been reduced
to only 10 to 15 percent in
the newer versions of silver
metal clays such as PMC+ and
the newest PMC3 formulas.
Art Clay shrinks even less,
at 8 to 10 percent. For most
jewelry pieces, shrinkage
can be advantageous when
working with design details.

Consider shrinkage when
adding other objects such as
fine-silver wire, CZs, or other
natural gems. The metal clay
will shrink around the added
element, making it appear
larger b-c].

Shrinkage will be a factor
when joining fired metal clay
with unfired metal clay. As
the metal clay shrinks during
firing, the already fired
portion will dome or buckle.
This can be an interesting
effect if you plan for it.

Shrinking rings
Metal clay shrinkage becomes
more of an issue when making
rings [d], particularly simple
band rings or bezels for
unusually shaped natural
gems. When it is necessary
to figure out the shrinkage
for a simple band, use the
calculations in the chart,
above right.

Determining shrinkage
The thickness, width, and
shape of the piece will effect
the shrinkage. Use the chart
at right as a guide to predict
how much a silver band will
shrink. To further understand
shrinkage, when you make a
band, take careful notes of
your process and refer back to
them as needed.

Follow these steps to make
a ring that will fit just right.
1. Wrap a strip of paper
around your finger (or
whatever object you want
the silver band to fit around
so that it fits comfortably.
Make a mark where the paper
begins to overlap (point a).
2. Unwrap the paper and
measure how long the final
silver band needs to be.
3. Weigh the metal clay you
will use with a metric scale.
4. Determine the anticipated
shrinkage (see chart, above
right), add that length to the
original length, and make a
second mark on the paper
strip (point b). For example,
if you are using 6g of metal
clay, you need to plan for
3mm of shrinkage. Mark your
strip 3mm beyond the first
mark you made.
5. Use the "Rolling snakes"
technique on page 23 to
gradually roll the metal-clay
lump into a snake reaching
point b.
6. Wrap the moist metal-clay
snake around the mandrel or
other object just to where the
two ends meet. Dry and sand.

calculating the shrinkage

Use this chart as a general guide
to predict the shrinkage of low-
fire metal clays.

Weight (g)	Shrinkage (mm)
3	1.5
4	2
5	2.5
6	3
7	3.5
8	4
9	4.5
10	5
11	5.5
12	6
13	6.5
14	7
15	7.5

*NOTE: The measurements above
are for bands up to 4.5mm wide.
For bands 5 to 8mm wide,
increase shrinkage by an
additional 1mm. For bands 9 to
12mm wide, increase shrinkage
by an additional 1.5mm.*

Adapted from *Silver Accessory, 1 Day
Handmade Series*, by Yusuke Nakamura,
SS Communications, Kadokawa Shoten
Group, 2002, ISBN 4827541159.

Because fine silver is softer
than sterling, it is possible to
make slight adjustments after
firing. A band ring can be
placed on a ring mandrel
and hammered lightly with
a leather mallet to stretch
the metal.

Burnishing

Now comes the magical part! With burnishing, the gleam of fine silver will appear—yes, it really is silver! After the metal-clay piece is fired, it will appear chalky white. To get the shiny finish, the surface particles of silver need to be pressed down, aligning the crystals. This process is called burnishing. It's like pressing snow down to a glassy ice surface. There are several ways to burnish.

Burnishing with a brush
Using a soft brass brush **[a]** with fine bristles, dip the brush in water and gently brush the piece. You will immediately begin to see a shine. This is a good way to achieve a soft satin shine.

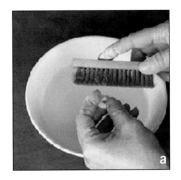

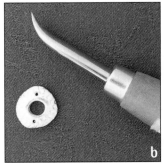

Burnishing with a handheld metal burnishing tool
With a hard metal burnishing tool **[b]**, you can create sparkling highlights by pressing down on select spots. This is a great way to bring out the texture of a piece and create contrast between satin and shiny finishes **[c]**.

Polishing
Polish your fired metal clay by hand. Start with 400-mesh then move on to 8000-mesh polishing papers. This will bring out a rich shine. Use sets of 3M Wet or Dry or Tri-Mite Polishing Papers.

Using an electric tumbler
Use a rock tumbler with stainless-steel shot and a liquid burnishing compound (be sure to follow the manufacturer's directions). Simply drop your pieces into the tumbler and tumble for 15 minutes to an hour to achieve an even shine. This is the fastest and easiest way to burnish several pieces at once.

Finishing with a shine
As the last step, polish each piece with a polishing cloth to bring out a warm glow.

Adding patina

If you'd like to add subtle shades of color, try using a patina after you've fired and burnished your metal-clay piece. Avoid getting patina on your burnishing tools or in your tumbler. **Photo a** shows a piece with no patina (left) and one with a liver of sulfur patina (right). Liver of sulfur is very easy to use.

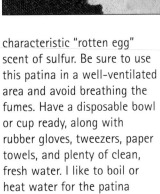

Patina colors
The interaction of various factors—the temperature of the patina solution, the length of time the piece is dipped and rinsed, and even the texture of the fired piece—creates unpredictable and delightful shades of gold, copper, pink, purple, blue, and grey. If silver is left in a patina solution too long, it becomes a dark pewter color. For a blacker look, you can try a silver oxidizing solution. Take care to read the safety precautions before using any of the patinas.

Buying liver of sulfur
Liver of sulfur comes in two forms—liquid and dry chunks in a can. You don't need very much. Liver of sulfur loses its effectiveness with time, so don't buy large quantities! Store liquid liver of sulfur in a cool, dark place.

Safety precautions
As soon as you open the bottle or can, you will smell the characteristic "rotten egg" scent of sulfur. Be sure to use this patina in a well-ventilated area and avoid breathing the fumes. Have a disposable bowl or cup ready, along with rubber gloves, tweezers, paper towels, and plenty of clean, fresh water. I like to boil or heat water for the patina solution and use cold running water to rinse the piece.

Using liver of sulfur
Place a pea-sized chunk of dry liver of sulfur in a small amount of hot water (just enough to cover the metal-clay piece). As soon as the chunk has melted, dip the metal-clay piece in the hot patina solution using tweezers. Colors will begin to appear in just a few seconds. As soon as you reach the desired color, rinse the piece in cold water. Repeat, if desired. Finish with cold water. Dry it with a paper towel and then use a polishing cloth to remove some of the patina and bring back the glow **[b]**.

Playing with polymer

Don't be fooled by this modest, inexpensive material. Polymer clay is a wonderful way to add color and texture to a metal-clay piece. See some of the leading polymer clay books and jewelry magazines to appreciate the wide range of fine work produced by today's leading polymer clay artists. Wendy Wallin Malinow makes wonderful, intricate designs combining polymer clay and metal clay.

Polymer clay can be added to finished metal-clay pieces, then baked following the directions for polymer clay without harming the silver.

Using polymer clay with metal clay

After the metal clay is fired and burnished, apply a small amount of glue, such as Sobo glue, to the surfaces where the polymer clay will attach. Let the glue dry until the surface is tacky, apply the polymer, and then bake the whole piece according to the directions provided by the polymer clay manufacturer. When creating the metal-clay piece, consider leaving rough surfaces that the polymer will be able to grip onto.

Polymer clay has its own characteristics, which make it different from glass and other colored material. Unlike glass, polymer clay does not shrink or flow. It can be used on very thin sheets of metal clay [a], the insides of metal-clay cylinders [b], both sides of metal-clay pieces, and with several colors next to each other without walls.

When using any of the methods described here, fill the cavities firmly with polymer clay so the polymer is slightly above the level of the metal clay. Bake according to the instructions for the polymer clay, taking into account the size and thickness of the piece. Fine silver conducts heat very well, so there is no need to add extra baking time. Take care not to burn the polymer clay!

Preparing polymer clay

Unlike metal clay, polymer clay needs to be conditioned before using. Using your hands is the easiest way to condition it but a pasta machine is a convenient way to condition polymer clay and make sheets of even thicknesses.

The pasta machine and any other tools used to condition or handle the polymer clay must not be used for food preparation or for metal clay work. Clean your hands well before handling the unfired metal clay. Unfired metal clay that's been contaminated by particles of polymer clay will be stained after firing.

Faux cloisonné

Polymer can be placed between metal-clay walls (or veins). The walls can be formed with stamps, whether they be rubber or carved, baked polymer stamps, or they can be carved directly out of a metal-clay base. Alternatively, cloisonné walls can be made with metal-clay syringe.

Faux champlevé

This is a way of adding color to cavities in metal clay. Roll out two metal-clay layers. Using very small "cookie cutter" type tools or a craft knife, cut out shapes in one layer. Let both layers dry until the cut shapes stay firm. Combine the two layers by completely covering the touching surfaces with metal-clay slip. After firing, burnishing, and polishing the metal-clay pieces, use polymer clay to fill in the cut-out designs.

Finishing polymer clay surfaces

After the piece cools, begin sanding the polymer clay with 300- or 400-grit sandpaper. Keep sanding until the polymer clay is at the same level as the metal clay. Buff with a muslin wheel on a Dremel tool or simply rub vigorously on a cotton cloth (like your jeans!). Then, using a cotton cloth or a buffing wheel, buff the piece until a smooth shine appears. If you use a buffing wheel, be sure to keep the piece moving across the face of the wheel so you do not gouge the clay.

Ceramics and metal clay

Low-fire metal clays can be wrapped around or painted onto unglazed bisque ceramics, such as this round bead [a]. The metal clay needs to be of an even thickness so it won't split as it shrinks during firing. On unglazed bisque beads, apply at least three layers of slip. Ceramics need to be heated and cooled slowly so they don't crack from thermal shock.

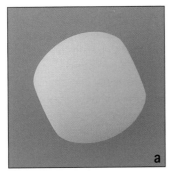

Colored ceramics
Glazed porcelain pieces can be wrapped with metal clay, which will adhere to the surface as it shrinks. Blue and white glazed pieces seem to

work best [b]. Other colors may discolor with the heat. If you are in doubt about whether a certain ceramic piece will work, try firing it alone. If it can withstand one firing, most likely it will withstand another.

Using metal clay with glazed ceramics
Art Clay® Silver 650 Overlay Paste will bond with glazed porcelain [c], unlike most of the other metal clays. Dry the metal clay completely before firing.

Fire in an electric kiln. Ramp up slowly, taking 60 minutes to reach the required

temperature. When finished firing, leave the kiln door closed and let it cool to room temperature.

Glass and metal clay

Low-fire metal clays can be combined with glass in many beautiful ways, but glass is sensitive, requiring an electric kiln to control the heating, and cooling rates. Because an in-depth discussion of combining glass with metal clay is outside the scope of this book, be sure to research the topic more before starting such a project. The web sites and publications listed in "Resources and suppliers," p. 125 are good places to start.

Using dichroic glass
Dichroic glass shimmers with wonderful colors and depth. Cabochons [a], or cabs as they are often called, need to be embedded in metal-clay slip or otherwise surrounded by metal clay so that the they stay in place [b]. Glass will fuse with metal clay but, for security, it's best to make sure you have a solid connection. Dry the clay completely and clean the surface of the glass before firing. Firing temperature, ramp speed,

and annealing requirements will depend on the glass type as well as size and thickness of the cab.

Fire a 1-in. cab in a low-fire metal-clay piece by ramping the kiln to 1500°F per hour. Hold at 1290°F for 10 minutes. Keep the kiln door closed and let cool to room temperature.

Adding lampworked glass to metal clay
This advanced technique requires knowledge of lampworking glass. To make a bead like the ones shown here [c], place a fired and burnished metal-clay spool [d] on the end of a rod, then wrap the hot, lampworked glass around the spool, burnish, and finish.

Cloisonné technique
Enamelling is a beautiful art form with an impressive history. Freshly fired and burnished metal clay is a perfect platform for glass enamel [e] because the surface is clean and ready to hold the enamel powders [f].

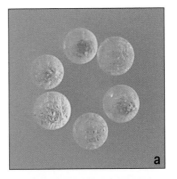

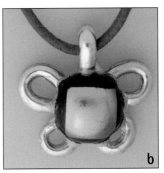

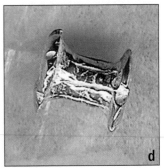

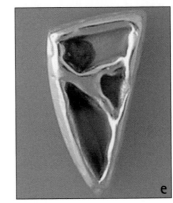

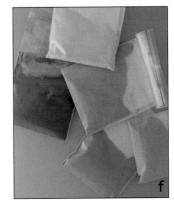

The enamel powders need to be prepared fresh each time you use them because they do not keep well. Transparent enamel powders need to be washed [g] first to get rid of fine particles which cloud the glass. Add about ¼ cup of water to 1 tablespoon of the powder, stir, and pour out the cloudy water. Repeat several times. Dry the washed enamel, sift in a 60 mesh enamel sifter to separate out the different sized granules, and mix the finer granules with clear-fire solution diluted with an equal amount of distilled water. Using a small paintbrush, apply a thin layer of enamel solution to a walled off space in the finished metal-clay piece. Avoid mixing different colors within one space and always use a separate brush for each color. After this layer has dried, place the piece in a hot kiln (1500°F kiln) for 3 minutes. When you see that the glass surface is shiny, remove the piece from the kiln to cool. The enamels are applied, dried, and fired one layer at a time.

Making an enamel/metal clay hybrid
It is also possible to mix enamel powders with metal clay to make a silver/glass hybrid. Equal parts of enamel and metal clay are kneaded together to create this interesting material. The finished metal clay shimmers with the enamel colors but it is also more brittle than metal clay alone. Check "Resources and suppliers," p. 125, to see examples of this work.

Using other types of glass
More possibilities exist with other forms of glass such as sea glass, glass seed beads, and sheets of colored glass. Art Clay® Silver Overlay Paste can be used to paint silver designs onto glass or to attach silver pieces to glass

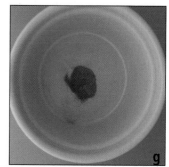

(see "Renaissance glass vase," p. 68). The process is similar to that for ceramics. In any work with glass, be aware of heating and cooling the piece at a slower rate than you would with metal clay alone. Glass is sensitive to changes in temperature and will crack, so be patient!

Easing into gold

Fired high-karat gold metal clay results in pure gold that is softer than 14K or 18K gold. The rich color [a] looks wonderful, especially against silver with a patina applied.

Characteristics of gold metal clay
Unfired gold metal clay is brown in color and is similar in consistency to silver metal clays. It can be handled just as you would handle silver clay; you can mold it, texture it, dry it, carve it, and fire it in a kiln. But gold clay fires at a higher temperature than silver clay. PMC® gold metal clay fires at 1830° F for 2 hours. Art Clay Gold 22k should be fired at 1813° F for 60 minutes.

PMC® Gold shrinks 25 to 30 percent and Art Clay® Gold shrinks 15 percent. This characteristic, along with the soft nature of pure gold, makes it impractical to use gold clay by itself for ring shanks or pieces that must endure stress. Gold metal clay is much more expensive than the silver clay.

Gold metal clay products
New paste-type gold metal clay products have been introduced. Mitsubishi's Aura 22 [b] and Art Clay World's Accent Gold for Silver—24K Paint are two types that are readily available. One way to use these products is to paint the gold onto fired silver pieces, dry, torch fire, and burnish. Follow the manufacturer's instructions for firing time and temperature. Other gold paste formulas may be available through on-line suppliers.

Using gold metal clay with silver metal clay
If using the lump form of gold metal clay, mold, texture, and fire the gold element first. Build the silver around the gold element and fire again at the lower temperature for firing silver metal clay.

Painting with gold metal clay
Many artists like to apply a small amount of gold metal clay to silver metal clay. One way to do this is to paint gold metal-clay slip onto clean,

just-fired, unburnished silver clay with a fine-point brush that is dedicated to use with gold. The gold clay can be thinned with water. Apply two or three thin layers of gold, allowing the piece to dry between each layer. It is best to torch-fire, rather than kiln-fire, with this method. Be sure that the gold slip has fused onto the silver by following the directions for torch firing. Burnish, patina, and polish as you would silver metal clay.

Keum-boo technique
Keum-boo, a technique in which pure gold and fine silver bond permanently through heat and pressure, is based on an ancient Korean metalworking method. Celie Fago describes this method thoroughly in her book, "Keum-Boo on Silver." Keum-boo can be used to apply gold paste or thin gold sheets [c] onto clean, just-fired, unburnished silver metal clay [d].

Use a small electric hotplate which can reach 900°F/480°C (many hotplates do not go this high). Judi Anderson of the PMC Guild has noted that this method produces a brighter gold color than kiln-firing does. The gold and silver will bond at temperatures

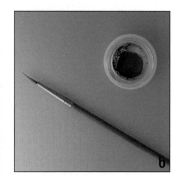

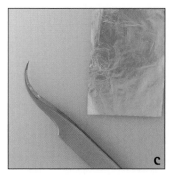

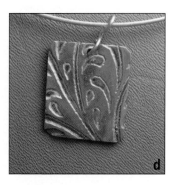

between 650°F and 850°F. A thermometer which can measure up to 900° F is useful. Other tools to have include leather gloves (it gets hot!), a steel or agate burnishing tool, wooden toothpicks, and a wooden holding stick (chopstick or popsicle stick is fine).

Paint a thin layer of gold paste or place a piece of gold sheet on the clean, just-fired silver metal clay. To help keep the gold sheet in place, you can apply a tiny drop of Elmer's ® School Glue Gel. Place the work on the hotplate and set the heat at 650°F or torch fire. With Aura 22 gold paste, apply two layers, dry, then torch

fire. Hold for one minute when the gold attains a soft red glow (only visible in a darkened room). As it heats up, the binder in the gold paste will begin to smoke (this is a harmless vapor). The piece must heat up enough for the gold to fuse to the silver. You can test this by pressing a wooden toothpick against the silver. If the wood chars, it is hot enough. While the metal is still hot, press the gold paste or gold sheet area with a burnishing tool. Hold the silver piece down with the holding stick in one hand while you rub with the burnishing tool in the other hand. Be sure to wear gloves!

You can repeat the process to deepen the color.

If the surface texture is uneven or there are deep grooves which make it difficult to use the burnishing tool, torch fire. or raise the hotplate temperature to 900°F (480°C) and let the silver piece sit for 30 minutes.

Allow the work to cool and then finish as you would silver metal clay by hand burnishing, or tumbling, and polishing. A patina can be used to increase the contrast between the silver and gold.

Gold sheet vs. gold paste
You can use the same Keum-boo technique with either gold sheet or paste but the

two forms have different characteristics and will produce different effects. You can cut shapes out of the gold sheet using paper punches or scissors, but first sandwich the delicate gold foil between two sheets of paper to avoid accidental tears. Gold sheet works best on lightly textured surfaces while gold paste can be applied to deeply textured surfaces. The foil will tear if it's used over sharp grooves.

Beginner metal clay projects

Once you become familiar with the basic process that turns

metal clay from a material that looks a lot like ordinary modeling

clay into a hard, shiny, custom-designed piece of precious metal

jewelry, you will be looking for ways to learn more about what

you can do with this exciting new medium. The projects on the

following pages will allow you to add one technique after another

to your personal toolbox as you experiment with shaping, carving,

texturing, stenciling, stamping, layering elements, and finishing.

These projects continue to be popular with those who take my

workshops and I hope they'll help inspire you as well.

Silver swirl pendant

This simple design is elegant and easy. Take time when you sand the surface before you fire the clay in order to achieve a smooth finish and wonderful shine. For this project, I used the metal clay Hot Pot kiln (see page 31). As you go through the steps for this project, feel the metal clay and experiment with its shape. Often the most interesting pieces come unexpectedly. You can always start over if you don't like the shape or the texture of your final piece.

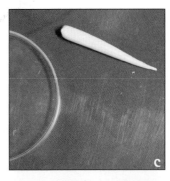

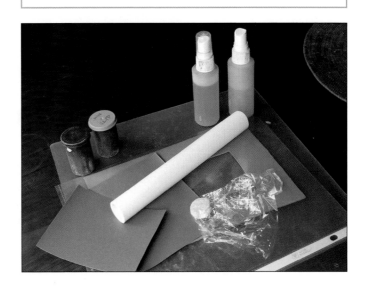

A beautiful
gleaming swirl

1 Use roundnose pliers to bend a 2-in. (5cm) piece of 18-gauge fine-silver wire into a loop for the bail [a]. Smash, twist, or press lines into the ends of the wire to rough them enough for the metal clay to grip.

2 Open the metal clay packet, take out a piece the size of a macadamia nut, and immediately wrap the unused portion of the metal clay in heavy plastic wrap. Store in an airtight container or seal back in the original package. Roll the clay into a ball, then place a lightly oiled plastic lid over the metal clay [b].

3 Roll out a tapered snake. It should be thinner on one end [c]. Keep it moist by covering it with plastic wrap.

4 Immediately shape the clay snake into a swirl. Press the bail into the moist metal clay so that the wire ends are completely covered [d]. Do not worry at this time if the area around the bail is rough. Let the metal clay dry.

5 Use a clay shaper or a small plastic makeup brush to fill in any gaps around the bail with metal-clay slip [e]. Let the clay dry.

6 Support the brittle metal clay with three fingers of one hand while you sand with the other. Start with 400-grit sandpaper and progress to 600-grit sandpaper or finer. Brush off any particles with a soft brush. Finally, use a damp makeup or paintbrush to smooth the entire surface [f]. The more time that you spend finishing and polishing the piece at this stage, the more brilliant the shine will be. Let the clay dry.

7 Fire the piece using a Hot Pot kiln, butane torch, or electric kiln (see pages 31-33).

8 Use a soft brass brush to burnish the piece. For more shine, burnish it and then polish it with a polishing cloth. You can also put it in a tumbler with stainless-steel shot and a burnishing compound for at least 30 minutes.

what you will need

- tools for working with metal clay, pages 11-13
- PMC3 or Art Clay 650
- PMC3 or Art Clay 650 slip
- 2 in. (5cm) 18-gauge fine-silver wire
- smooth plastic lid or piece of Plexiglas
- roundnose pliers
- wire cutters
- burnishing tools, page 14
- silver chain for necklace (optional)
- Hot Pot kiln, butane torch, or electric kiln

Before you begin, review the following sections:
- Metal-clay slip, page 21
- Working with fine-silver wire, page 28
- Drying metal clay, page 29
- Carving and sanding metal clay, page 30
- Burnishing, page 37

Beginner metal clay projects

This project provides a good introduction to making textured flat pieces and using a stencil. The heart is a simple shape to start with. A stencil makes it easier to select an area of the flattened metal clay to cut. Using a stencil also allows you to cut multiple pieces that you know will be uniform. After mastering this process, experiment with different shapes—stars, moons, and other, more challenging designs. Now you can wear your own heart on your sleeve!

 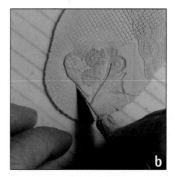 

1 Design and cut out the heart stencil.

2 Roll out a flat, even piece of metal clay. Texture the clay as desired. Keep the metal clay moist by keeping it inside the plastic sheet protector as you roll it and whenever you are not working with the clay.

3 Choose a section of the textured metal clay to be used for the pin and gently press the stencil into the clay [a]. Cut out the shape with a craft knife [b]. Dry the heart.

4 Sand and smooth the edges [c]. Remember to support the piece with three fingers as you sand—the dried metal clay is brittle and can easily be broken. Leave the back rough where the pin back can be glued later.

5 Fire the piece using a Hot Pot kiln, butane torch, or electric kiln (see pages 31-33). When the piece cools from the firing, burnish it using a fine-bristle brass brush. Use a burnisher for a glossier finish, or place the piece in a tumbler with stainless-steel shot and a burnishing compound. Patina, if desired, and polish with a polishing cloth.

6 Use a glue suitable for metal which will dry clear such as a two part epoxy. Glue pin back in place and let dry overnight until the glue is clear.

what you will need

- tools for working with metal clay, pages 11-13
- PMC3 or Art Clay 650
- stencil paper or a playing card
- rubber stamp, lace, leaves, or other texturing materials
- Hot Pot kiln, butane torch, or electric kiln
- burnishing tools, page 14
- liver of sulfur (optional)
- pin back finding
- E6000 or other adhesive

Before you begin, review the following sections:
- Rolling out a flat piece, page 19
- Texturing rolled-out flat pieces, page 20
- Stencils, page 21
- Drying metal clay, page 29
- Burnishing, page 37
- Adding patina, page 37

A simple yet

charming pin

Thanks to their handcrafted yet modern look, these earrings are appropriate for the office as well as a night on the town or other special occasion. Textured disks set in rims turn freely on silver wires that loop from earring posts.

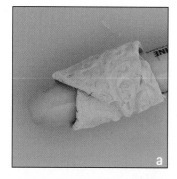

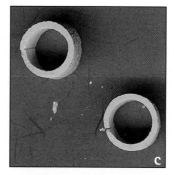
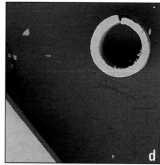

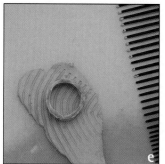
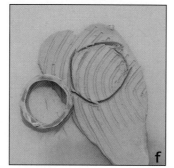
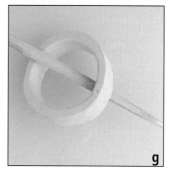
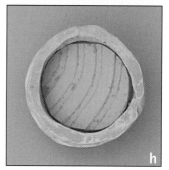

1 Metal clay dries out quickly, so work rapidly to shape it. Keep it moist by covering the piece with plastic wrap if you must stop. Have your textures ready, and oil the pen or other cylindrical support form.

2 Wrap the textured metal clay slab around the cylinder form [a]. While it is moist, use a playing card or tissue blade to cut two wheels about the same width [b]. Do not worry if the edges are ragged; you will smooth them after the pieces are dry.

3 Allow the clay to harden a few minutes, then remove it from the cylindrical form to dry completely [c].

4 Smooth the ends of the two pieces by gently sanding in a circular motion on sandpaper laid flat on the table [d].

5 Place the ends of the dried and sanded wheels on a layer of textured metal clay [e]. Gently cut along the outside of the wheel [f]. (The clay will shrink as it dries, so you need to cut out wet clay

pieces on the large side.) You should have two circles which are about the same size. Dry the two discs.

6 Gently sand the edges of all four pieces with the emery board and needle tool in a curving motion so that all surfaces are rounded and smooth [g]. Try fitting the two pieces together [h]. As soon as the discs can fit inside the wheels, apply a small amount of metal-clay slip to the inside of the wheel and press the discs to the center. Fill in any gaps around the edges with more metal clay and let dry.

7 Gently drill a hole into each disc with a needle sanding tool. Make sure the silver wire will fit loosely through the holes.

8 Fire the pieces using a Hot Pot kiln, butane torch, or electric kiln (see pages 31-33).

9 When the earrings are cool, burnish them and then tumble them if you want a high-gloss finish. Add a liver of sulfur patina if you desire.

what you will need

- tools for working with metal clay, pages 11-13
- PMC3 or Art Clay 650
- PMC3 or Art Clay 650 slip
- cylindrical form with ½-in. diameter, such as a fat marking pen
- texture tools
- Hot Pot kiln, butane torch, or electric kiln
- burnishing tools, page 14
- tumbler with stainless-steel shot and burnishing compound (optional)
- liver of sulfur (optional)
- 6 in. (15cm) 18-gauge fine-silver wire
- roundnose pliers
- wire cutters
- pair of earring findings

Before you begin, review the following sections:
- Rolling out a flat piece, page 19
- Texturing rolled-out flat pieces, page 20
- Creating a cylinder, page 23
- Working with fine-silver wire, page 28
- Burnishing, page 37
- Adding patina, page 37

10 Use wire cutters to cut the silver wire in half. Use roundnose pliers to make a small loop at the end of one of the pieces.

11 Put the silver wire through the finished silver wheels and twist the ends. Attach the completed wheels to the earring findings.

A simple geometric design

Give yourself plenty of time to carve and polish this piece. Choose a shape that will be meaningful for you. In this project, I use fine-silver wire as a frame around which I apply the metal clay. Keep in mind that any metal, including fine-silver wire, hardens as you work it. For best results, therefore, have a design in mind from the start so you can shape the wire with minimal handling.

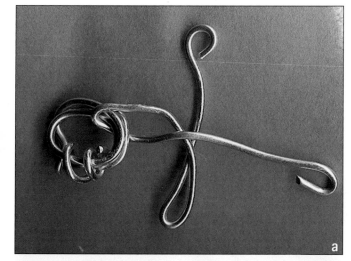

Make a hand-crafted, one-of-a-kind piece

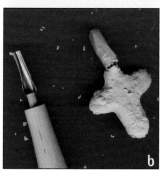

1 Use inexpensive craft wire first to work out your wire-support design, then build a skeleton with fine-silver wire. Wrap more wire through the top loop of the skeleton to make a bail [a]. If the wire hardens too much to work, heat it with a torch until you can work it again.

2 Press the moist metal clay onto the skeleton firmly. Avoid any air bubbles. Use the rubber-tipped clay tool to completely cover the wire, except for the bail. (Tape the bail to keep it from falling into the moist clay.) Smooth out the surface. Let dry until it is leather hard.

3 Support the piece with one hand while you use the carving tool in the other hand to gently start carving out small pieces [b]. You can try another design on the other side to have different looks with one piece. Remember to work over a plastic sheet so that you can collect the shavings to put in a slip container [c].

4 Use a soft brush to remove any particles. Fire the piece using a Hot Pot kiln, butane torch, or electric kiln (see pages 31-33). If the pendant is large, you can refire the piece or extend the firing time to ensure complete firing. Burnish and patina [d].

what you will need

- tools for working with metal clay, pages 11-13
- PMC3 or Art Clay 650
- 8 in. (20cm) 16-gauge fine-silver wire
- roundnose and chainnose pliers
- wire cutters
- Hot Pot kiln, butane torch, or electric kiln
- burnishing tools, page 14
- liver of sulfur

Before you begin, review the following sections:
- Working with fine-silver wire, page 28
- Carving and sanding metal clay, page 30
- Burnishing, page 37
- Adding patina, page 37

Layering textures allows you to create an elegant, multi-dimensional design using techniques easy enough for those new to working with metal clay. Adding a cubic zirconia (CZ) stone creates a sparkle of color. Use the techniques learned in earlier projects to create the background layer, the loop, and the top appliqué piece with the gem. Using different textures on the appliqué and background pieces will focus more attention on the appliqué. Simply varying the size of this project will enable you to turn it into a treasured ornament, a pendant for a necklace, or weighted ends on a ribbon bookmark.

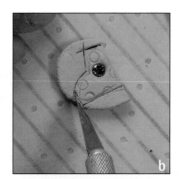

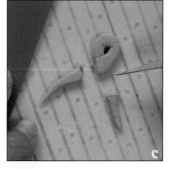

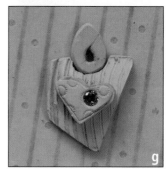

1 Design and cut out two stencils: one for the top appliqué (here, a heart) and the other for the background. Roll out to flatten a piece of metal clay, then texture it. Cut out the heart design and the background piece [a].

2 Add the cubic zirconia (CZ) stone to the moist top piece. Dry both pieces [b].

3 Roll a snake of moist metal clay with your hands, a plastic lid, or a piece of Plexiglas. Curve it into a loop, and cut off the ends [c]. Flatten the loop with the roller. Let dry, then sand the loop with strips of sandpaper or a needle file [d].

4 Turn the background piece facedown. Place the rolled-snake loop about halfway into the bottom piece. Mark the position with a pencil. Using an X-acto knife or carving tool, gently carve out a notch for the loop. Dried metal clay is similar to chalk in consistency, so use small movements to carve it.

5 After all the pieces are dried and sanded, place the bottom piece facedown on a small platform (a playing card is fine). Put a small amount of thick slip into the notch, then press the loop into the notch [e]. Apply more slip on the seam between the notch and the loop. Allow the piece to dry [f].

6 Turn the background piece faceup. Apply slip in the middle of the back of the top appliqué piece. Gently press onto the bottom piece. Dry completely [g]. Fire, burnish, and add patina.

7 Fire the pieces, using a Hot Pot kiln, butane torch, or electric kiln (see pages 31-33). Burnish, then add patina.

what you will need

- tools for working with metal clay, pages 11-13
- texturing tools
- stencil paper or a playing card
- PMC3 or Art Clay 650
- PMC3 or Art Clay 650 slip
- 4mm CZ, must be kiln-firable
- tools to handle CZ
- Hot Pot Kiln, butane torch, or electric kiln
- burnishing tools, page 14
- liver of sulfur

Before you begin, review the following sections:
- Rolling out a flat piece, page 19
- Texturing rolled-out flat pieces, page 20
- Stencils, page 21
- Metal-clay slip, page 21
- Layering, page 22
- Rolling snakes, page 23
- Firing with cubic zirconias page 35
- Burnishing, page 37
- Adding patina, page 37

Create wonderful

textures with layering

Make an assortment of hollow beads to add a personal touch to your beaded jewelry. In the following two pages, I'll show you how to make two different types of hollow beads—cylinder beads and sandwich beads. Cylinder beads are just what their name implies—beads formed from a cylinder of metal clay. Sandwich beads start as three textured, flat metal-clay pieces which are sandwiched together with metal-clay slip. Experiment with shapes and add decorative touches to create your own trademark beads. Finally, string them together or with various other beads to make a unique bracelet.

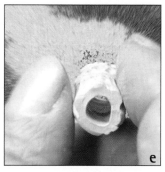

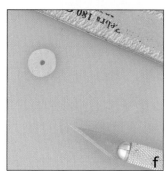

what you will need

- tools for working with metal clay, pages 11–13
- texturing tools
- PMC3 or Art Clay 650
- PMC3 or Art Clay 650 slip
- plastic drinking straw or other tubular support form
- burnishing tools, page 14
- tumbler with stainless-steel shot and burnishing compound (optional)
- Hot Pot kiln, butane torch, or electric kiln
- plastic lid or Plexiglas to roll decorative balls
- liver of sulfur (optional)
- assorted glass, metal, or gemstone beads (optional)
- 12 in. (31cm) flexible beading wire
- clasp
- crimp beads (amount needed depends on design)
- flatnose or chainnose pliers
- wire cutters

Before you begin, review the following sections:
- Rolling out a flat piece, page 19
- Stencils, page 21
- The sandwich method, page 22
- Creating a cylinder, page 23
- Rolling snakes, page 23
- Carving and sanding metal clay, page 30
- Burnishing, page 37
- Adding patina, page 37

Cylinder beads

1 Because metal clay dries out quickly, you need to shape it before cracks begin to appear. Oil the texturing pieces and the straw or other cylindrical support form. Roll out and texture the clay [a].

2 Wrap the clay around the cylinder [b]. While the clay is moist, slice through the overlap and slice off the rough ends with a playing card or tissue blade [c]. Remove the scraps and gently pinch the seam together. Let the cylinder dry just enough to hold its shape [d]. Slide it off the straw. Use a small brush to add slip to the inside of the seam. Dry completely.

3 Smooth the ends of the bead by gently sanding in a circular motion on the sandpaper laid flat on the table [e].

4 If you would like your cylinder bead to have closed ends, cut out two disks wider than the diameter of the bead. Make small holes with a sharp tool. Dry them separately [f].

5 Use metal-clay slip to join the dried end caps to the cylinder. Dry and sand the joints. Widen the holes with a round needle file.

6 If the bead can stand on its end, fire standing on a flat surface. If it cannot, fire in vermiculite or a fiber blanket.

7 Burnish the bead. Apply a patina if desired. Polish with a polishing cloth.

Sandwich bead

1 Decide on the textures and shape of the bead. Roll a piece of clay to the thickness of five playing cards and texture it.

2 Make a stencil into the shape you want your bead to be. Use the stencil to cut out three metal-clay pieces. Choose one of the pieces to be the middle piece and cut it in half. Allow the pieces to dry.

3 When dry, gently carve out the center of each half of the middle piece [see photo g, p. 56].

4 Stack the pieces together, facing the carved-out sides of the middle piece toward each other. After

continued on the next page

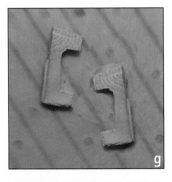
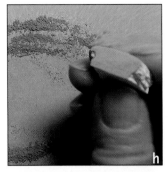
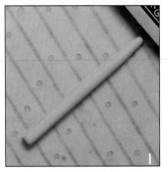
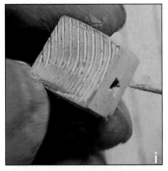

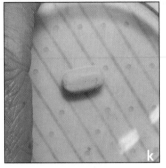
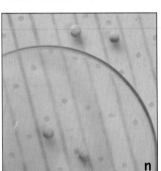

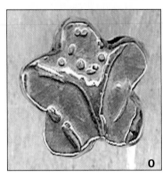
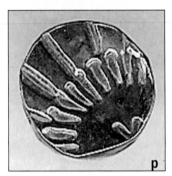

Combine basic cylinder and sandwich beads in a truly handmade bracelet

making sure they fit together, apply a generous amount of metal-clay slip between the layers and dry again.

5 Sand the sides of the bead smooth with sandpaper or an emery board, starting with the coarsest grit and finishing with a fine grit [h]. Use a needle file to make and round out the holes [i].

6 To make decorative silver balls like the ones on the bead pictured in **photo j**, take a small piece of moist metal clay and use a flat, clear plastic or Plexiglas sheet to roll it into a snake [k-l]. Cut the snake into equally-sized pieces [m]. Roll again to create individual round pieces [n]. Make extras in case some are the wrong size or shape. Avoid losing these slippery little pieces by placing them

in a bottle cap or lid. Let the balls dry completely.

7 Apply a generous amount of slip to the bead. Use the tweezers to place each dried ball on the slip. Let dry. Sand and remove excess metal clay. Use fine sandpaper to smooth out undesired cracks or imperfections on the decorative balls.

8 Finish as in steps six and seven of "Cylinder bead" on the previous page. See [o] and [p] above for examples of finished sandwich beads.

Make a bracelet

1 Determine the desired length of your bracelet. Add 5 in. (13cm) and cut a piece of flexible beading wire to that length.

2 Arrange your beads as desired. To make an exposed-wire bracelet like those shown on page 54, put the beads in groups of one to seven beads. Space the groups ¼–½ in. (6.4mm-1.3cm) apart. Place a crimp bead on each end of the bead groups.

3 String a crimp bead, a 2mm glass or metal bead, and one clasp part 3 in. (7.6cm) from one end of the beading wire. Go back through the beads with the tail and flatten the crimp bead with flatnose or chainnose pliers.

4 If making a bracelet without exposed wire, string a few beads over the wire and the wire tail. Trim the excess wire from the tail. String the rest of the beads as

well as a crimp, a 2mm bead, and the other clasp part. Go back through the 2mm bead, the crimp, and a few more beads. Snug up the beads, leaving a bit of ease, and flatten the crimp bead.

5 If making an exposed-wire bracelet, string a bead group on the beading wire. Be sure to go over the short tail and trim any excess wire. Flatten both crimp beads to hold the group in place. String the rest of the bead groups in the same manner, leaving space between groups.

6 When all the bead groups are strung, string a crimp, a 2mm bead, and the other clasp part. Go back through the 2mm bead and the crimp bead. Flatten the crimp bead and trim any excess wire.

Combine a sparkling cubic zirconia with a simple shape to make a stunning pendant you'll wear for years. This project starts with three components: a cubic zirconia (CZ) set in a metal-clay bezel, a fine-silver wire loop, and a rolled snake that joins the pieces together into a cohesive whole. To highlight the elegant design, take the time to sand the surface as smooth as possible before firing. The compliments you're sure to receive will make the extra effort well worth it. Choose your favorite color CZ or alter the shape of the pendant to put your personal spin on this classic.

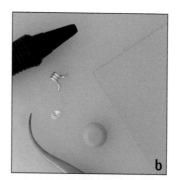

a

b

c

d

e

f

A simple and elegant design

1 Wrap a 3-in. (7.6cm) piece of fine-silver wire one or more times around a circular form, like a wooden skewer or toothpick, to make a bail for the necklace chain or cord to go through. Leave "legs" to anchor the wire in the metal clay [a]. Roughen the legs by flattening and slightly curving them.

2 Have your tools at hand [b] so you'll be able to work quickly. Roll a small amount of metal clay into a ball on a Plexiglas surface. Use tweezers to immediately place the cubic zirconia (CZ) point-side down on the ball. Use the tip of a retracted ballpoint pen to gently press the CZ deep into the clay to leave room for sanding. Set aside and allow to dry.

3 Use a sheet of Plexiglas to roll a "snake" slightly thinner than the width of the bezel piece [c]. Trim the ends of the snake at an angle so that they fit well against the bezel. Use metal-clay slip to quickly join the ends to the bezel [d]. Now take the silver wire bail and press the legs into the soft clay [e]. The pendant will look rough at this stage. Let dry completely.

4 To smooth the pendant, fill in the seams and any imperfections with metal-clay slip [f]. Let dry. Take your time as you sand the entire surface smooth. Sand the pendant on a flat piece of sandpaper. Use a needle file or a strip of sandpaper to sand the inside of the pendant. [g]

5 Use a needle file to gently carve away the metal clay at the back of the CZ [h]. This will allow light to shine through the CZ, enhancing the sparkle. Use a damp makeup brush to smooth the entire surface [i]. Let dry.

6 Use a toothpick to remove clay from the surface of the CZ [j]. Brush away any remaining clay dust with a makeup brush.

7 Fire at the temperature required for PMC3 or Art Clay 650. Do not quench the fired piece or remove it from the kiln right away—this will crack the CZ. Let the pendant cool slowly in the kiln to room temperature. Take time as you burnish [k] to bring out a high shine.

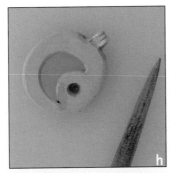

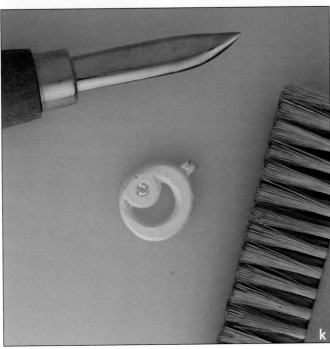

what you will need

- tools for working with metal clay, pages 11-13
- PMC3 or Art Clay 650
- PMC3 or Art Clay 650 slip
- 3 in. (7.6cm) 18-gauge fine-silver wire
- roundnose pliers
- wire cutters
- cubic zirconia (CZ)
- tweezers
- retractable ball point pen
- electric kiln
- burnishing tools, page 14

Before you begin, review the following sections:
- Rolling snakes, page 23
- Working with fine-silver wire, page 28
- Firing with cubic zirconias, page 35
- Carving and sanding metal clay, page 30
- Burnishing, page 37

Silver bookmark

Use rubber stamps with words or other flat textures to make a special bookmark that's as sturdy as it is beautiful. You can use any flat texture such as leaves, rubber stamps, bottle caps, or lace. After texturing the clay, cut out your favorite portions, make loops to hang them from, and tie them securely to the ends of a chain or a sleek leather or satin cord.

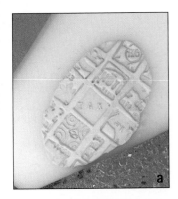

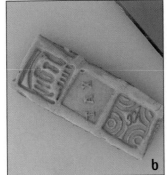

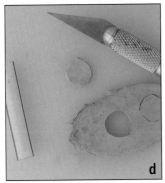

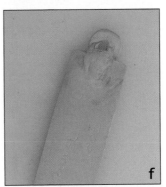

A special gift for

your favorite

book lover

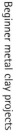

1 Roll out and texture a piece of metal clay that is five or six playing cards thick [a]. With a tissue blade or craft knife, cut out two pieces a little larger than the size you want the finished bookmark pieces to be [b]. Select pieces which have lettering, if you desire. Dry.

2 Use an emery board to sand the edges of the two pieces [c]. Set aside.

3 To make the loops, roll a piece of metal clay out to the same thickness as the bookmark pieces. Use a large drinking straw to cut out two loops [d]. Use a small cocktail straw to make a hole in the center of each loop.

Dry and sand. Use a needle sanding tool or thin strips of sandpaper to sand the loops. Don't forget to sand the inside of the loops also.

4 Sand one side of a loop flat. Attach it to a bookmark piece with metal-clay slip [e]. Place facedown on the support cards. Use more slip to cover the seam on the back [f]. Allow to dry completely. Repeat with the second piece.

5 On the back of the larger piece, inscribe a message with a pencil, if desired. Use a sharp tool to scratch along the pencil lines. Brush off dust with a makeup brush.

what you will need

- tools for working with metal clay, pages 11-13
- PMC3® or Art Clay® 650
- PMC3® or Art Clay® 650 slip
- rubber stamp or other flat texture
- Hot Pot kiln, butane torch, or electric kiln
- burnishing tools, page 14
- liver of sulfur (optional)
- 12 in. ribbon, chain, or leather cord

Before you begin, review the following sections:
- Rolling out a flat piece, page 19
- Texturing rolled-out flat pieces, page 20
- Burnishing, page 37
- Adding patina, page 37

6 Fire flat. When cool, burnish with a hand burnishing tool and wire brush [g] to bring out a high glow [h]. Apply patina if desired.

7 Cut a 12-inch piece of leather cord, ribbon, or chain, and tie one part of the bookmark to each end.

Beginner metal clay projects

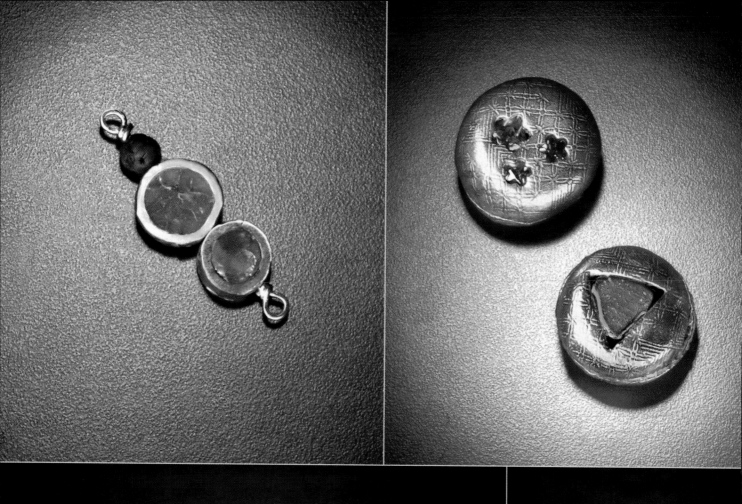

Intermediate
metal clay
projects

Now that you're familiar with the basic metal clay skills—

rolling, texturing, layering, shaping, and finishing—it's time to get

acquainted with more techniques. You'll learn how to make a mold

from a favorite button or unusual object, how to incorporate

polymer clay into a metal-clay piece, and three fool-proof ways

to make metal-clay rings with a perfect fit. The projects in Chapter 4

are varied: jewelry, a pillbox, a pet tag, and more. Whether you plan

to make these items for yourself or to give them as gifts, you'll find

this assortment appealing.

This fun project introduces you to building a three-dimensional design using flat textured pieces. The trickiest part is "gluing" the six pieces together. If it is too difficult to do all at once, do one joint at a time, letting it dry between each step. Be sure to use an index or playing card as a platform to work on. This allows you to move the entire platform rather than trying to pick up individual pieces of clay.

a

b

c

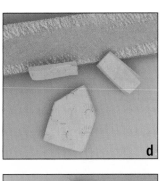

d

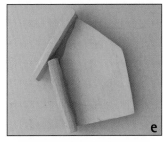

e

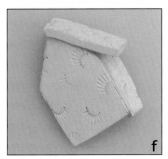

f

1 Design and cut out the stencils. Make the house design first. Then measure and make the roof piece longer to make eaves. Measure and make the side of the house. You need to make only three stencil shapes since two metal-clay pieces will be made from each stencil [a].

2 Roll out and texture the metal clay.

3 Use the stencils to cut out the house pieces. Cut out two pieces (for front and back) from the house-shaped stencil. Cut out two side pieces and two roof pieces. Using an X-acto knife, cut out a door and a window from one of the house pieces [b].

4 Dry all the pieces flat [c]. Sand and smooth all edges including the little door and window. Remember to support each piece as you sand—the dried metal clay is brittle. In order to fit the pieces together, bevel the edges by sanding with an emery board [d].

5 Use a clay shaper tool or a small makeup brush to apply thick metal-clay slip to attach the sides of the house to the front. Let dry, then attach the back [e]. Dry again before attaching the roof pieces. Apply more slip on the inside of the house to strengthen the joints [f]. Dry again.

6 Trim and sand the outside of the house. If the house will be a pendant, use the X-acto knife or a needle file to carve out two small holes in the upper part of the roof where a cord can be strung.

7 Fire and burnish. Add patina if desired. If the house will be a pin, use a glue suitable for metal. Glue pin back and let dry overnight until clear.

---

what you will need

- tools for working with metal clay, pages 11-13
- PMC3
- PMC3 slip
- playing card to make stencil
- Hot Pot kiln, butane torch, or electric kiln
- burnishing tools, page 14
- liver of sulfur patina (optional)
- chain or cord for necklace (optional)

Before you begin, review the following sections:
- Rolling out a flat piece, page 19
- Texturing rolled-out flat pieces, page 20
- Stencils, page 21
- Metal-clay slip, page 21
- Burnishing, page 37
- Adding patina, page 37

Wear this sweet

miniature house

as a pin

or a pendant

Intermediate metal clay projects

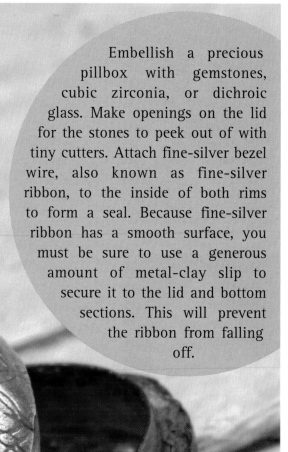

Embellish a precious pillbox with gemstones, cubic zirconia, or dichroic glass. Make openings on the lid for the stones to peek out of with tiny cutters. Attach fine-silver bezel wire, also known as fine-silver ribbon, to the inside of both rims to form a seal. Because fine-silver ribbon has a smooth surface, you must be sure to use a generous amount of metal-clay slip to secure it to the lid and bottom sections. This will prevent the ribbon from falling off.

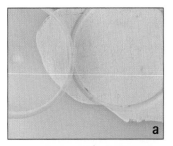
a

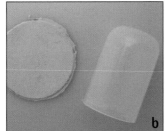
b

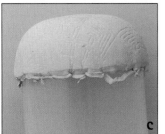
c

d

e

f

g

h

Make a pretty, stylish box to hold your small treasures

what you will need

- tools for working with metal clay, pages 11-13
- PMC3 or Art Clay 650
- PMC3 or Art Clay 650 slip
- texturing material
- rounded plastic cap with straight sides to use as a support form (here a lotion bottle cap)
- circle template that is 30 percent larger than the diameter of the support form
- 1/4-in.-wide 18-gauge fine-silver bezel wire (also known as fine-silver ribbon): twice the length of the inner diameter of the support form
- kiln-firable gemstones (such as CZs or glass) that will fit inside the holes made with tiny cutters or craft knife
- Hot Pot kiln or electric kiln
- burnishing tools, page 14
- patina (optional)

Before you begin, review the following sections:
- Rolling out flat pieces, page 19
- Texturing rolled-out flat pieces, page 20
- Metal-clay slip, page 21
- Firing with cubic zirconias, page 35
- Burnishing, page 37
- Adding patina, page 37

1 Roll out metal clay to an even thickness of four or five playing cards. Texture the clay lightly [a].

2 Cut out two circle-shaped pieces, about 30 percent larger than the diameter of the plastic support form [b]. Keep these pieces moist under a plastic sheet protector.

3 Lightly oil the end of the plastic support form with olive oil to keep the metal clay from sticking. To make the bottom of the box, take a moist metal clay circle and gently wrap it around the end of the form [c].

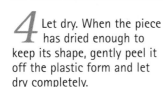
i

4 Let dry. When the piece has dried enough to keep its shape, gently peel it off the plastic form and let dry completely.

5 To make the top of the box, take the second moist metal-clay circle and wrap it around the plastic form. Use a small pattern cutter to cut out shapes from the moist clay [d]. Let dry as the first piece was dried.

6 Sand both metal-clay pieces. Gently support the piece with three or four fingers. Sand in a circular motion on sandpaper laid flat on the table [e]. Use needle files to sand the inside edges of the cut-out designs also.

7 Support the pieces with vermiculite or a fiber blanket and fire. Do not burnish when cool.

8 Cut two lengths of 1/4-in.-wide silver bezel wire so that they will fit inside the lid and the bottom piece [f]. Using the tweezers, place the glass cabs or gemstones facedown inside the cutouts on the inside of the lid [g]. Apply a generous amount of metal-clay slip to hold the stones in place and fill gaps. Let dry. Apply more slip if necessary.

9 Slightly roughen the edges of the bezel wire. With metal-clay slip, attach a strip of silver bezel wire to the inside of each piece [h]. Make the diameter of one a bit smaller than the other so that it can fit inside the other. Add more slip along the edge of the bezel wire [i]. The metal-clay slip will shrink around the bezel wire during firing, forming a tight seal.

10 When the pieces are completely dry, use a toothpick to gently rub any metal clay off the faces of the gemstones.

11 Fire again, air cool, and burnish. Patina, if desired, and polish.

Intermediate metal clay projects

67

Use Art Clay Silver Overlay Paste to attach bezeled CZs to a glass vase. Make the bezels first with PMC3 or Art Clay Silver 650 and then attach them to the glass with thin coats of the paste. To prevent cracks, allow the vase to cool slowly in the closed kiln after firing.

Get the look of
the Renaissance
from a small
glass vase and
cubic zirconias

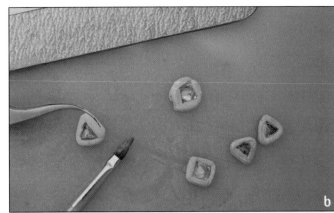

1 To make bezels with gemstones inside, roll round pieces of moist metal clay and press the CZs flat-side down into the clay so the point of the stone sticks out of the clay. Press the moist bezels onto the glass vase. Let dry [a].

2 Remove the dried bezels from the glass. Sand and shape the dried bezels [b]. Use an emery board to sand each side of the bezel. Sand further with wet/dry sandpaper and fine sandpaper, and then go over the surface with a damp paintbrush to smooth. Use a toothpick to smooth the inside edges of the bezel and remove any metal clay on the surface of the CZ [c]. In the photo, note the difference between the just-pressed bezel on the left and the one which is sanded and cleaned on the right.

3 Fire the bezels with CZs at the temperature required for PMC3 or Art Clay Silver 650. Let cool in the kiln to avoid cracking the CZs. Do not burnish.

4 Using the rubber-tipped clay shaper or a small makeup brush (keep brush end in water to prevent drying out), apply a generous amount of Art Clay Silver Overlay Paste on the back of the fired bezel. Press each bezel onto the glass vase and dry [d]. If desired, apply two or more coats of overlay paste on the rim of the vase [e].

5 Use a toothpick to trim away any excess paste and clean the surface of the CZs. Be sure to leave enough paste around each bezel so that the paste can grip the bezel [f].

6 Fire the entire vase at 1200°F (650°C) for 30 minutes. Let the vase cool in the kiln, keeping the lid closed. Burnish with a brass brush and hard burnishing tool. Apply a patina if desired.

what you will need

- tools for working with metal clay, pages 11-13
- small heavy glass bottle or vase
- 5 or more kiln-firable CZs
- PMC3 or Art Clay Silver 650
- Art Clay Silver Overlay Paste
- toothpick
- electric kiln
- burnishing tools, page 14
- patina (optional)

Before you begin, review the following sections:
- Firing with cubic zirconias, page 35
- Burnishing, page 37
- Adding patina, page 37

Silver wire ring with ornament

Make this easy ring by attaching a molded metal ornament to a wire band. Because the band is wire instead of metal clay, you won't need to worry about shrinkage—just make the band to fit your finger. If you don't want to mold the ornament piece, simply roll out a thick flat piece of metal clay and texture it.

a

A beautiful
first ring

b

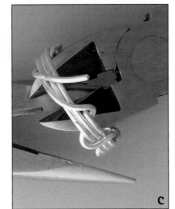

c

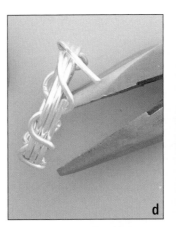

d

e

f

1 Make a mold of the ornament you want to use. In this case, I used an inexpensive plastic button and a molding compound. Let the mold set while you begin the ring band.

2 Use a strip of paper and tape to make a ring which fits comfortably on the finger and is easy to get on and off. Tape the paper ring closed. Place the paper ring on a ring mandrel and mark the wider spot on the mandrel with a pencil [a].

3 Wrap the silver wire around the mark on the mandrel three times [b]. Use small, roundnose pliers to wrap the tail of the wire around the three bands to hold them together. Cut the wire so that the ends meet and they both can be covered by the ornament [c]. Slightly bend or smash the ends of the wire with pliers so that they will grip the metal clay ornament and not slip out.

4 Use flatnose pliers to slightly flatten all four ring band wires [d]. Make sure the wrapping wire is flattened against the rest of the band. Try the wire ring on. It should be a little loose at this point so you will have room for the ornament piece.

5 To make the ornament, press a lump of metal clay firmly into the mold to ensure there are no air pockets [e]. Immediately pop the piece out of the mold by gently bending the mold. Avoid handling the piece and distorting the moist ornament. Place it faceup on a playing card to dry [f]. If you are using a flat piece for the ornament, place it on the mandrel or your paper ring and press it gently so it curves.

continued on the next page

---

what you will need

- tools for working with metal clay, pages 11-13
- PMC3 or Art Clay 650
- PMC3 or Art Clay 650 slip
- 15 in. (38m) 18-gauge fine-silver wire
- roundnose and flatnose pliers
- wire cutters
- button or other item to mold for ring ornament
- two-part silicon mold compound
- ring mandrel
- Hot Pot kiln, butane torch, or electric kiln
- burnishing tools, page 14
- liver of sulfur (optional)

Before you begin, review the following sections:
- Making a mold, page 28
- Working with fine-silver wire, page 28
- Burnishing, page 37
- Adding patina, page 37

Intermediate metal clay projects

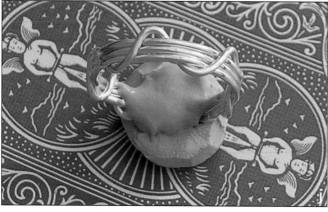
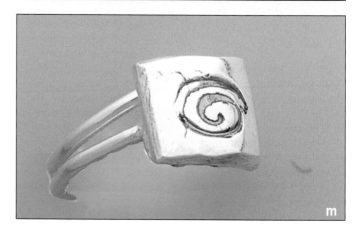

6 Dry faceup inside a warm toaster oven for a few minutes. The surface should be hard but the inside should still be slightly moist and soft.

7 Trim any excess clay from around the edges with a craft knife [g] and carve a groove in the back of the ornament [h] where the silver wire band will fit in. Place the band into the ornament to be sure the wire ends will be covered inside the ornament and there will still be room for your finger [i]. Dry thoroughly.

8 Sand all edges smooth and dry the ornament completely. Be sure there is nothing which will catch on clothing or skin.

9 Place the ornament facedown on a playing card. Paint slip into the carved indentation in the back of the ornament. Then gently place the wire band, wire ends down, into the slip [i]. Add more slip to cover the wire ends. Avoid trapping air in the slip. Carefully place the card with the ring on it in a warm toaster oven to dry completely.

10 Using a rolled up piece of sanding paper or a needle sanding tool, gently sand the inside of the ring so that it will fit comfortably [k].

11 Fire in the metal clay Hot Pot kiln [l]. Finish as usual. Use liver of sulfur to add a patina, if you desire. You can adjust the shape of the ring by placing it on the mandrel and gently pressing or pounding it with a leather mallet to avoid scratching it.

Photo **m** shows a wire band ring with a textured flat ornament rather than a molded one.

Two-part ring

Both the band and the ornament of this bold ring are made with metal clay. The pieces are made and fired separately and then put together and fired again. This makes a certain amount of adjustment possible. Texture the band as desired. Buttons and old coins are ideal for molding the ornament. Or, instead of using a mold to make the ornament, you can simply rubber stamp or otherwise texture a thick (at least eight cards taped together) piece of rolled metal clay.

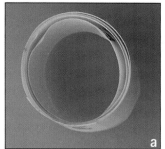

a

b

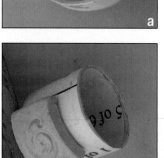

c

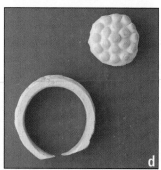

d

e

edges. Use a needle file or an emery board to sand and smooth the edges of the ornament. Gently try the ring band on your finger. The ring band should be loose.

5 Fire the two pieces separately. Do not burnish. Try on the fired ring band. It should fit more snugly than before but still be a little loose to allow room for the clay which will attach the ornament. If the band needs to be bigger or smaller, gently press the band with both thumbs to adjust. Fine silver is softer than sterling, so this will not be difficult to do.

6 Place the ornament facedown on a support platform such as a playing card. If it doesn't balance, support it with cellophane tape. Apply thick metal-clay slip on the back of the ornament. Place the ends of the ring band into the slip. Apply more slip to cover the ring band ends [e]. Dry completely.

7 Gently try the ring on. It should fit now. If needed, smooth the inside of the ring, particularly where the ornament joins the band. Use rounded sandpaper or needle sanding tools.

8 Fire. Burnish, add patina, and polish.

Make a substantial ring with a bold ornament

1 Begin by making a paper ring. Roll a strip of paper around your finger so that it fits comfortably and will slide over the knuckle. Tape closed. To allow for shrinkage, wrap the paper strip four more times around the paper ring and tape again (if you have large fingers, make an additional two or three wraps) [a].

2 Choose textures to use on the ring band. Roll out a flat piece of metal clay about five cards thick and texture it. Wrap this flat metal clay around the paper ring so that the ends overlap. Use a playing card to cut one edge of the moist metal clay. Cut in a circular motion around the paper ring [b]. Cut the other edge in the same manner and then cut through the overlapped clay portions. Store the scraps with other clay. Dry on the paper ring until it is just hard enough to hold its shape, then gently slide the metal clay off the paper ring so that it can dry thoroughly.

3 Make the ring ornament by using the two-part molding compound, or simply roll and texture another flat piece of metal clay that is at least six playing cards thick. Place the moist ornament on the paper ring so that it is slightly curved [c]. Dry in the same way the band was dried.

4 Carefully sand the band and the ornament. To smooth the sides of the ring band, hold it with three fingers and sand in a gentle circular motion against sandpaper that is laid flat. Sand the ends of the ring band down so they are flat [d]. The ornament should fit over the tapered ring band ends. Round the edges of the band so there are no sharp

what you will need

- tools for working with metal clay, pages 11-13
- PMC3 or Art Clay 650
- PMC3 or Art Clay 650 slip
- two-part silicon molding compound
- heavyweight copy paper
- cellophane tape
- Hot Pot kiln, butane torch, or electric kiln
- burnishing tools, page 14
- liver of sulfur

Before you begin, review the following sections:
- Rolling out a flat piece, page 19
- Texturing rolled-out flat pieces, page 20
- Metal-clay slip, page 21
- Making a mold, page 28
- Burnishing, page 37
- Adding patina, page 37

Open ring

If you want to have a little flexibility in a ring's size, this is a good design for you. The band remains open, providing a little give. With a core of silver wire, the ring band is strong and flexible. Take your time when sanding the dried piece to give it a nice, smooth finish.

If you do not have a mandrel, you can still make this ring. Roll up several sheets of paper to create a stiff paper mandrel. Make the paper mandrel in a cone shape so that you can find the exact size you want.

a

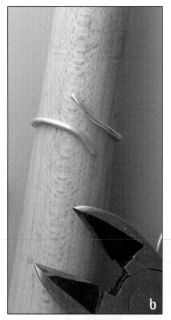

b

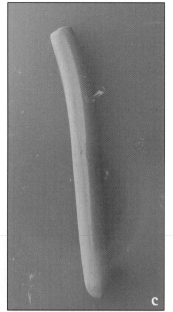

c

d

A strong yet flexible ring design

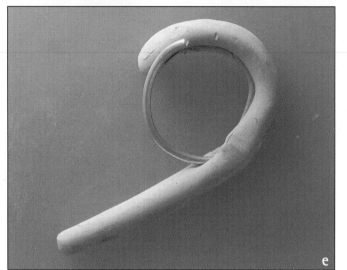

e

f

1 Prepare the mandrel. If you don't have a wooden ring mandrel, try making a paper mandrel. To do so, take three sheets of paper and roll them together into a cylinder with one side narrower than your ring size and the other side wider. Tape both sides **[a]**.

2 To find your ring size, take a strip of paper and wrap it around your finger so that it slides comfortably over the knuckle. Tape the paper. Slide it on the mandrel and mark the wider spot with a pencil or pen.

3 Wrap the silver wire around the mandrel at the marked spot. If you do not have a hard mandrel, wrap the wire around your finger. The ends of the wire should turn slightly away from each other **[b]**.

4 Use a plastic lid or piece of Plexiglas to roll a metal clay "snake" of an even thickness that is long enough to cover the silver wire ring **[c]**. Cover with plastic wrap to keep the band moist.

5 Gently wrap the soft metal clay snake around the silver wire **[d–e]**, being careful to cover the wire ends. Slide the ring back on the mandrel.

6 Texture the moist clay. Use a leather stamp or another small texture item to apply designs deep into the soft metal clay. Dry. The ring band will still be rough and the silver wire will be visible inside the ring **[f–g]**.

g

h

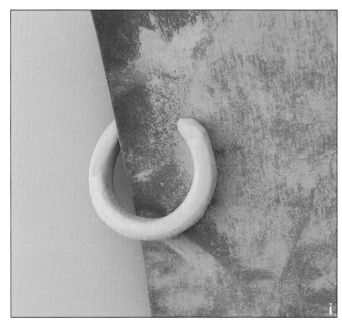

i

j

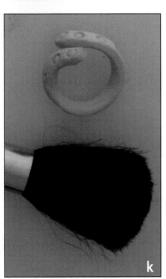

k

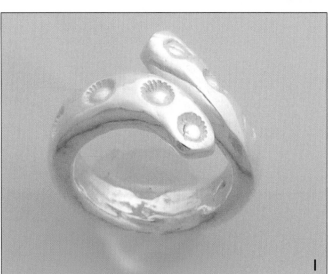

l

7 Sand the edges [h–i]. Apply thick metal-clay slip to cover the silver wire. Dry again. Roll the sandpaper to sand the inside of the ring [j]. Once the surface is smooth, gently dust with a soft makeup brush to remove particles from the deep grooves of the textures [k].

8 Place the ring on a bed of vermiculite and fire. Burnish and polish [l]. Apply patina if desired.

what you will need

- tools for working with metal clay, pages 11–13
- PMC3 or Art Clay 650
- PMC3 or Art Clay 650 slip
- 4 in. (10cm) 16- or 18-gauge fine-silver wire
- wire cutters
- small texture tools that make deep impressions
- ring mandrel or several sheets of thick paper to make one
- plastic lid or piece of Plexiglas
- Hot Pot kiln, butane torch, or electric kiln
- burnishing tools, page 14
- liver of sulfur patina (optional)

Before you begin, review the following sections:
- Rolling snakes, page 23
- Working with fine-silver wire, page 28
- Burnishing, page 37
- Adding patina, page 37

Ring band

This simple ring band is deceptively challenging. Even PMC3 and Art Clay 650 shrink, so if you want an exact fit, you will have to measure carefully and pay attention to the details. The thickness, width, and shape of the ring all affect how and how much it will shrink. Use the shrinkage chart on page 36 as a guide. Because fine silver is relatively soft, it's possible to make slight adjustments after firing by placing the ring on a mandrel and tapping it lightly with a mallet.

a

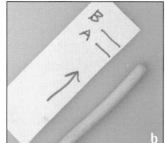
b

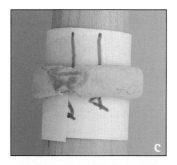
c

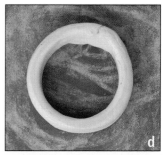
d

e

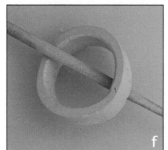
f

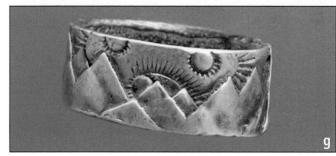
g

1 First, make a paper ring by winding a strip of paper around the finger so that it fits comfortably and slides over the knuckle. Mark the point where the paper strip meets as point A. Now you have a strip with your actual ring size marked.

2 Determine the shrinkage using a metric weight scale, the shrinkage chart on page 36, and a metric ruler. Take the amount of metal clay you wish to use and weigh it. Find the weight on the chart and see what the shrinkage will be. Add that amount to your ring size marked on the paper strip and make a new mark—point B [a]. Lay the strip flat on top of a plastic sheet protector.

3 Take the clay you just weighed and roll it gradually to the length of the second mark on your paper strip [b]. Slightly flatten the snake by pressing down on the Plexiglas. Keep the band moist under a piece of plastic.

4 Tape the paper strip at point B and slide it on the mandrel. Moisten the snake with a damp paintbrush if needed. Immediately wrap it around the paper ring on the mandrel. The ends of the snake should just meet.

5 Gently press the ends together just enough so it will stay in place [c]. Dry in a warm toaster oven for a few minutes. If the ring holds its shape, gently take it off the mandrel to dry thoroughly.

6 Apply metal-clay slip to join and cover the ends. Dry again. The dried ring should still be a loose fit on your finger.

7 Sand the ring. The more time you spend at this stage, the smoother the final surface will be. Start with medium-grit and progress to fine-grit sandpapers. Hold the ring with three fingers and use a circular motion to sand the two outside edges on sandpaper that is laid flat [d]. To sand the outside surface of the ring, move the emery board or the sanding papers around the ring in smooth strokes. To sand the inside, roll the sandpaper [e] or use a round or half-round needle sanding tool [f].

what you will need

- tools for working with metal clay, pages 11-13
- PMC3 or Art Clay 650
- PMC3 or Art Clay 650 slip
- metric weight scale
- metric ruler
- strips of paper
- ring mandrel or sheets of paper to make one (only a wood or metal mandrel will work if you need to adjust the size after firing)
- Hot Pot kiln, butane torch, or electric kiln
- small square of Plexiglas or a flat plastic lid
- burnishing tools, page 14
- patina (optional)

Before you begin, review the following sections:
- Rolling snakes, page 23
- Shrinkage, page 36
- Burnishing, page 37
- Adding patina, page 37

8 Use a soft makeup brush to remove fine particles. As a final step, use a damp makeup brush to smooth the entire surface.

9 Dry again. If desired, insert a heat-resistant form into the ring to help it maintain the correct size. Hattie's Patties work well. Check with the organizations listed in "Resources and suppliers," page 125, for availability. Fire. If the ring is slightly small, place it on a wooden mandrel and tap it wider with a leather mallet. Burnish and polish.

Photo g shows an example of this ring band decorated with textures, metal-clay paper, and patina [7].

Discover the

beauty of

simplicity

Using polymer clay is an easy way to add color, texture, and different effects to metal-clay pieces. In the two beads on the left, I used the mokume gane technique, originally a method used by Japanese metal-smiths to create the look of wood grain in metal. When applied to polymer, it creates deep swirls of color. You can also use solid colors or try rubber stamps with heat-set inks to add designs on the polymer clay surface.

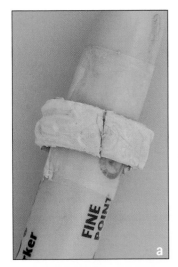

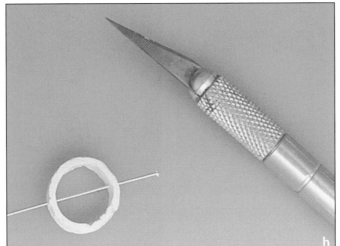

Be careful not to get any polymer clay on the unfired metal clay or the tools for metal clay, or unsightly stains will result. Work on the metal-clay pieces first, put away all metal clay tools, and begin firing the metal clay before opening the polymer clay packages. Keep tools separate and use polymer clay tools only for polymer clay.

1 Roll out and texture a piece of metal clay at least five cards thick. Cut the edges to form a long rectangle and wrap it around a cylindrical form to fashion a ring [a]. Seal with metal-clay slip to be sure the joint is secure.

2 Dry and sand. Drill small holes for stringing through the sides of the bead with a needle file, craft knife, or drill bit [b]. Fire and burnish [c]. After the cylinders are completely burnished and polished, insert a silver head pin into the holes in the cylinder. Set aside.

3 There are several brands of polymer clay: do not mix them. Read the baking instructions on the package and set your toaster oven to the correct temperature. (The toaster oven must be reserved for use with polymer clay only.) Be sure to have ventilation so that the fumes from baking polymer clay can be vented out.

Use your hands or a pasta machine at the #1 setting (the thickest) to knead and condition the polymer clay.

4 Prepare small amounts of three or four colors along with larger blocks of translucent clay [d]. Knead a portion of one of the colors into a piece of the translucent polymer clay [e].

continued on the next page

Color, texture,

and designs

framed

in silver

Intermediate metal clay projects

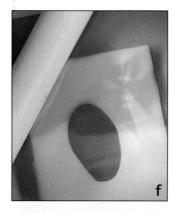

f

g

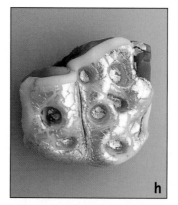

h

i

j

k

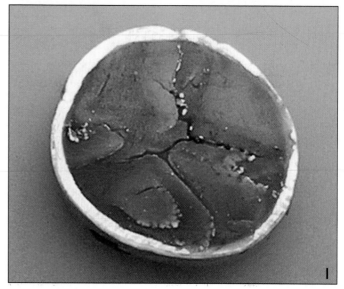

l

5 Use the plastic sheet protector, shim, and roller (or a dedicated pasta machine) to roll out thin slabs of each color of the polymer clay [f]. Cut each color sheet into squares.

6 Layer the different colors and the silver foil [g]. Press the stack down firmly to remove any air pockets.

7 Using the end of a pen, press random holes into the polymer clay [h]. Press the polymer clay into a solid block [i]. If the clay is very soft, wrap in plastic wrap and refrigerate for an hour.

8 Using a tissue blade, slice layers off the firm block of layered polymer clay. Use the shim, plastic sheet protector, and roller to press random polymer slices together into a mokume gane design [j].

9 Take the small pieces of the mokume gane and press firmly into the silver cylinders with the head pins inserted [k]. For a flat surface, let a small amount of polymer clay rise above the edge of the silver cylinder. Slide the head pin in the holes in the cylinder and move it a bit to widen the hole. Remove the head pin and place the cylinder on a baking sheet in a clay-dedicated toaster oven. Bake according to the manufacturer's instructions. To protect the piece from burning, place a sheet of white paper above and below it.

10 After the bead has cooled, sand the polymer clay surface in a bowl of water that you change frequently. Begin with 400-grit wet/dry and gradually work up to the highest grit sandpaper. Finish off with a muslin wheel mounted on a power drill or simply rub the piece vigorously on clean cotton cloth for a smooth finish [l].

what you will need

- tools for working with metal clay, pages 11-13
- PMC3 or Art Clay 650
- PMC3 or Art Clay 650 slip
- texture tools
- Hot Pot kiln, butane torch, or electric kiln
- burnishing tools, page 14
- polymer clay in three or four of your favorite colors and a block of translucent polymer clay
- silver leaf or foil
- toaster oven dedicated to polymer clay use
- tools for working with polymer clay
- baking sheet
- soft cotton buffing wheel
- head pins

Before you begin, review the following section:
- Rolling out a flat piece, page 19
- Texturing rolled-out flat pieces, page 20
- Creating a cylinder, page 23
- Burnishing, page 37
- Playing with polymer, page 38

Display your affection for your pet with this pendant. Put the pet's name or a special message on one side and your pet's paw print on the other side. Wear it yourself on a chain or hang it on your pet's collar and show the world how much you love your four-legged child.

Use fine-silver bezel wire, also known as fine-silver ribbon, to make a strong frame and bail to support the metal-clay body. Twisted or braided, fine-silver wire can be used in place of the bezel wire if desired.

a

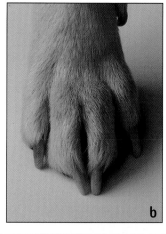

b

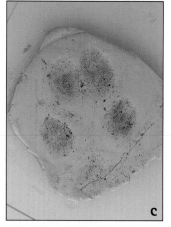

c

d

e

f

what you will need

- tools for working with metal clay, pages 11-13
- PMC3 or Art Clay 650
- PMC3 or Art Clay 650 slip
- a cooperative pet (preferably a little hungry)
- pet's favorite food
- ³/₁₆-in.-wide (4.76mm) fine-silver bezel wire, .33mm thick: enough to wrap around the fired pendant three times and make a small bail
- wire-working tools
- cellophane tape
- small flat ceramic plate
- Hot Pot kiln, butane torch, or electric kiln
- burnishing tools, page 14
- liver of sulfur (optional)

Before you begin, review the following sections:
- Rolling out a flat piece, page 19
- Metal-clay slip, page 21
- Burnishing, page 37
- Adding patina, page 37

Preserve your pet's
paw print in fine silver

1 Prepare to make the footprint imprint. Roll out a thick layer of metal clay about 15 playing cards thick [a]. Place the metal clay on a small, lightly oiled plastic sheet or plate. Cover with plastic wrap to keep moist.

2 I have found it easiest to make a footprint while my pet is eating. Place the moist metal clay under his or her foot [b]. Press the foot into the clay firmly. Immediately remove the metal clay. Place the metal-clay piece on a plate in a warm toaster oven until the piece is leather dry. The footprint should be hard, but the other side should still be slightly moist [c].

3 Remove the excess clay along the outside of the footprint. Flip to the other side. Pencil a sketch of what you want to write directly on the clay. Use a sharp tool or a fine carving tool to carve out deep grooves along the pencil lines [d]. Dry completely.

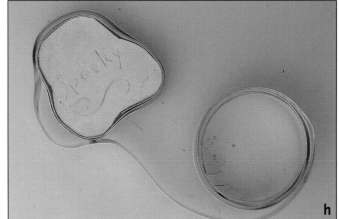

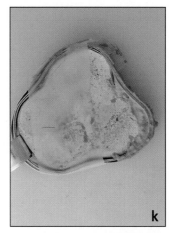

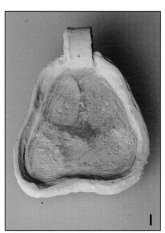

4 Place the footprint piece with the message side down on sandpaper [e]. Sand using circular motions. Sand down as much as possible so that the piece is about five playing cards thick. Carve the message again if necessary. Use a makeup brush to gently brush the metal clay particles out of the carved design [f]. Sand the edges smooth. Fire. Do not burnish.

5 To make the frame and bail, first make a foam rubber insert in the same shape as the footprint [g]. Use this insert to keep the footprint piece in place in the frame. Roughen the surface of the fine-silver bezel wire by scratching with a sharp tool and also sanding the edges. Wrap the wire around the footprint piece three times and cut the wire [h]. Use another piece of wire to make the bail by wrapping it around the frame three times [i].

6 Place the pendant with the foam insert into the frame [j]. Apply thick metal-clay slip to the frame to cover the edges [k]. Use tape to hold the ribbon end in place if necessary. Cover the seam between the pendant and the frame [l]. Dry. Remove the foam insert and tape. Apply more slip to the seam on the other side [m]. Dry again.

7 Remove excess clay from the pendant faces, sand the frame, and wipe the entire surface smooth with a damp makeup brush.

8 Fire the pendant in a bed of vermiculite. Burnish and add a patina, if you desire. Polish.

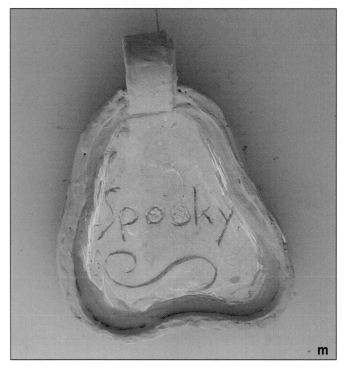

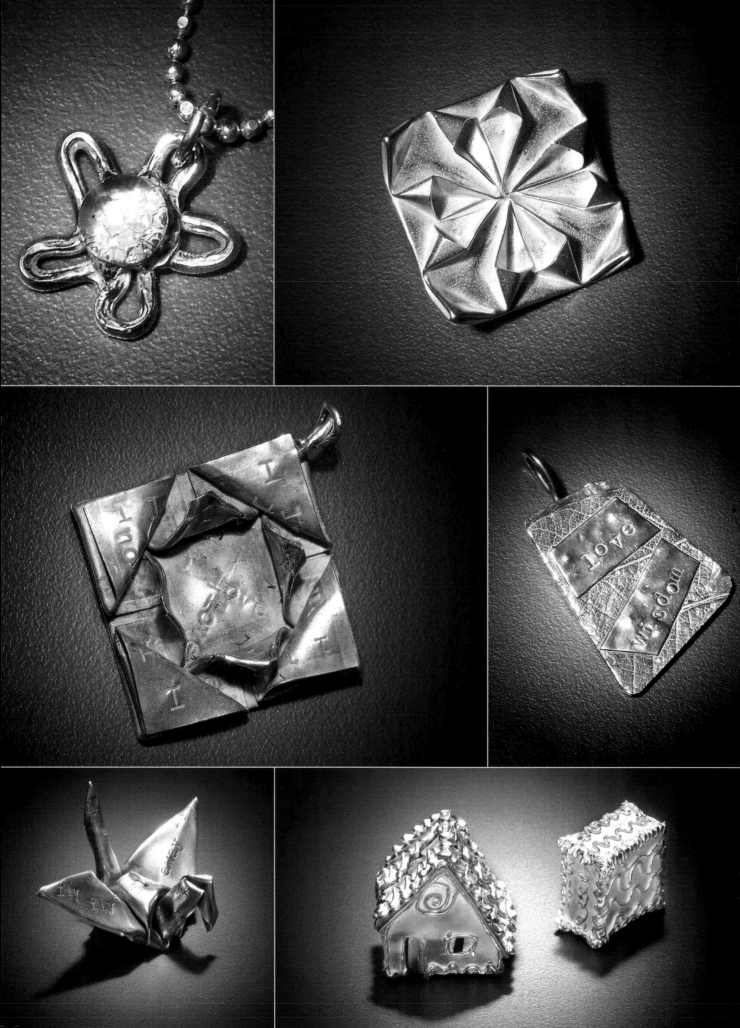

chapter 5

Working with metal-clay paper and syringe

So far, all of the projects in this book have been made from the lump-clay form of metal clay, occasionally held together with a little slip or paste. Two other forms of metal clay are also available, expanding the range of possible projects and components. Metal-clay paper and metal-clay syringe represent exciting developments in metal clay as they allow one to easily make folded or elaborately decorated pieces. In this chapter, I'll show you how to use these two types of clay in interesting ways, like making folded origami pieces, using syringe to make a form, and incorporating typewritten messages.

I like the look of old type—letters slightly askew and faded, like secret messages obscured by time. I use an electric typewriter to impress words directly into the metal-clay paper. Learn how to do this on page 24, "Working with metal-clay sheet or paper." Layering the metal-clay paper over a textured background makes the message stand out. Fire the metal-clay paper separately before adding the background piece to make sure the text is clear.

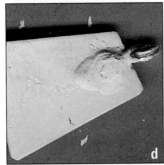

1 Type words or phrases on the metal-clay paper [a].

2 Trim the metal-clay sheet into strips containing one or two words each [b]. Fire at the temperature required for metal-clay paper.

3 Roll out a piece of metal clay to the thickness of five playing cards. Make it larger than you want your finished item to be. Texture it and cut it to the desired size and shape. Dry and sand.

4 To make a bail, cut a 2-in. (5cm) piece of fine-silver wire and hold it in the middle with a pair of roundnose pliers. Make a loop by wrapping the wire around one jaw of the pliers. Repeat with the other end to make another loop right next to the first, if desired. Leaving a ¼-in. (6.4mm) tail on each end, trim the excess wire.

5 Hold the wire bail against the back of the dried metal-clay piece to see how it will look from the front. Mark the location of the bail [c]. Apply some slip on the marks and place the bail in the slip. Apply more slip on top of the wire bail to cover the wire ends completely [d]. Take care not to trap air in the slip. Dry completely and sand smooth if needed.

6 Attach the fired word strip to the background piece [e]. Place a dab of thick slip in the center of the back of the strip. Press the strip onto the background piece and dry again.

7 Fire, burnish, and add patina if desired.

Add inspirational

messages to your

original jewelry

Working with metal-clay paper and syringe

89

Personalize a set of shakers or other porcelain items with metal clay. If you can, remove rubber stoppers and other parts before firing. In this case, the shakers had stainless steel tops glued on which would not come off. I fired them anyway. The tops came off as the glue burned away but they were discolored. I cleaned them with metal cleaning cream and glued them back on with industrial strength glue.

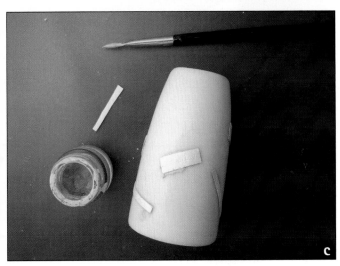

1 Remove caps and rubber stoppers from the shakers [a]. Clean surfaces well with dishwashing soap.

2 Texture and type on the metal-clay sheets. Cut the sheet to desired sizes [b]. Fire the pieces at the temperature required for metal-clay paper. Do not burnish yet.

3 Decide where the metal-clay paper strips will be positioned. Curve the sheets so that they will fit the porcelain form.

4 Use a rubber-tipped clay tool or a paintbrush to apply a generous amount of Art Clay Silver Overlay Paste to the fired sheets. Attach the strips to the porcelain shakers [c]. Allow some of the paste to extend beyond the sheet strips. This is necessary so that the paste can grip the sheet. Dry.

5 Using a toothpick, trim off any excess paste but leave a rim of the overlay paste around each sheet strip. Gently sand the surface of the dried paste. Fire at the temperature required for Overlay Paste. Allow the piece to cool to room temperature in a closed kiln.

6 Burnish with a brush. Apply liver of sulfur patina if desired [d].

what you will need

- tools for working with metal clay, pages 11-13
- porcelain salt and pepper shakers
- PMC+ Sheet or Art Clay Silver Paper
- typewriter or other texture item
- Art Clay Silver Overlay Paste
- electric kiln
- burnishing tools, page 14
- liver of sulfur (optional)

Before you begin, review the following sections:
- Working with metal-clay sheet or paper, page 24
- Burnishing, page 37
- Adding patina, page 37

Attach fine silver elements to porcelain with Art Clay Silver Overlay Paste

Origami, the
Japanese art of folding
paper, is a wonderful way
to use metal-clay paper.
Practice with origami paper or
cardstock first to understand
each fold. Metal-clay paper is
thicker than origami paper, so it's
trickier to fold the corners and
multiple layers. Avoid folding
metal-clay paper too hard or
often. Unlike the lump-clay form,
once metal-clay paper tears, it
cannot be repaired. After you
have mastered this project,
try the Silver Crane or
the many other designs
that origami
offers.

Origami star

Make sure your hands and work area are dry before working with metal-clay paper. Do not apply olive oil or hand balm to your hands prior to beginning this project.

In origami, many folds are made, then undone, either to guide future folds or to form creases that will help the piece take shape. Steps 1-3 demonstrate examples of this type of fold.

Begin with a square piece of metal-clay paper. The final folded piece will be half the size of the original sheet. Once fired, it will be somewhat smaller due to shrinkage. PMC+ Sheet comes as a 6cm (approximately 2³⁄₈ in.) square and is a good size for this pendant. If you choose to make earrings, you may want to cut the sheet down somewhat.

1 Fold the metal-clay square into a triangle [a]. Unfold [b] and then fold into a triangle the other way, using the other corners. Unfold again. You will have two faint lines going across the square.

2 Bring the four corners into the middle, using the faint diagonal lines as a guide [c].

3 Again, bring the four corners into the middle [d-e]. There are now four layers of metal-clay paper.

4 Unfold, leaving only two corners folded in [f]. Bring in the unfolded side to the center [g]. Unfold the other corners. Bring in the second side to make a rectangle [h].

continued on the next page

----

what you will need

- tools for working with metal clay, pages 11-13
- PMC+ Sheet
- electric kiln
- burnishing tools or tumbler, page 14
- pin back
- E6000 glue

Before you begin, review the following sections:
- Working with metal-clay sheet or paper, page 24
- Burnishing, page 37

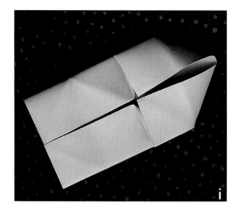

i

j

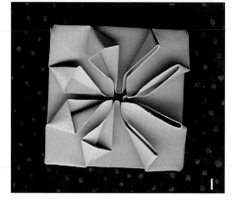

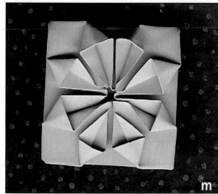

k

Capture the elegance of origami in fine silver

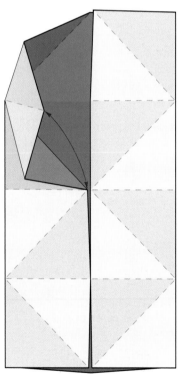

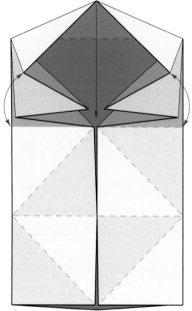

l

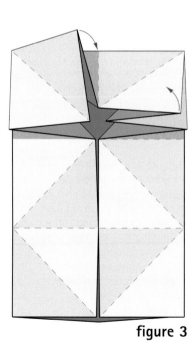

m

figure 1

figure 2

figure 3

n

o

5 Lift one corner and fold it down so that it points to the center of the sheet [figure 1]. Repeat with the other corner on this first end of the rectangle [i]. Holding the two corners in the middle of the sheet, begin to press the pointed end toward the middle. Do not fold it over directly, rather let the form unfold and flatten into a rectangle [figure 2]. Lift the two corners and fold them back along the fold lines to meet along the center line [figure 3]. Repeat on the other end of the rectangle, resulting in four squares which are open along the two center lines [j].

6 Take the open edges of one square and fold them in toward each other, making two "wings" [k]. Repeat with the edges of the other three squares. Open each of these wings and press flat [l–m].

7 Fire on a ceramic-fiber tile in an electric kiln at the recommended time and temperature for metal-clay paper.

8 Use E6000 adhesive to glue the pin back on. Let dry thoroughly. Burnish in a tumbler if desired.

Add a colorful sparkle to your star by including a beautiful CZ in the center. Make a hole in the corner through which you can string an earring finding [n], or turn the piece into a pendant [o] by adding a bail.

Adding color
After firing the star piece, follow the steps on page 35, "Firing with cubic zirconia," to make the bezel. Use metal-clay slip to join the bezel to the star.

Earring variation
The earrings pictured in **photo n** represent a variation on the star pin. Follow steps 1 through 5 to make the form shown in **photo j**. Instead of folding the edges of the squares toward each other, lift the point of each square and fold it back so it's pointing away from the center. Place a CZ inside the folds and fire. Poke a hole through one corner for the earring wire. Repeat to make a matching earring.

Making a bail
Make a bail with fine-silver wire (see "Message jewelry," page 88), lump-form metal clay (see "Silver bookmark," page 60), or metal-clay paper, as shown in **photo o**. In the pendant pictured above, I simply formed a strip of metal-clay paper into a loop, fired it, then attached it to the fired star with metal-clay slip. A final firing secured the bail to the pendant.

Origami crane

The origami cran[e] although a very popul[ar] origami form, is one of the mo[st] difficult ones to fold. If you a[re] new to origami, try practicing fi[rst] with origami paper. Then u[se] cardstock to get used to folding [a] thicker material. I use a vinyl-back[ed] fabric to demonstrate to my classes. Th[e] crane can be made into a penda[nt] or ornament by stringing it onto co[rd] or beading wire. Or make two smal[ler] versions, add a couple of beads, a[nd] attach them to earring wir[es.] Metal-clay origami is fun a[nd] the possibilities are endles[s.]

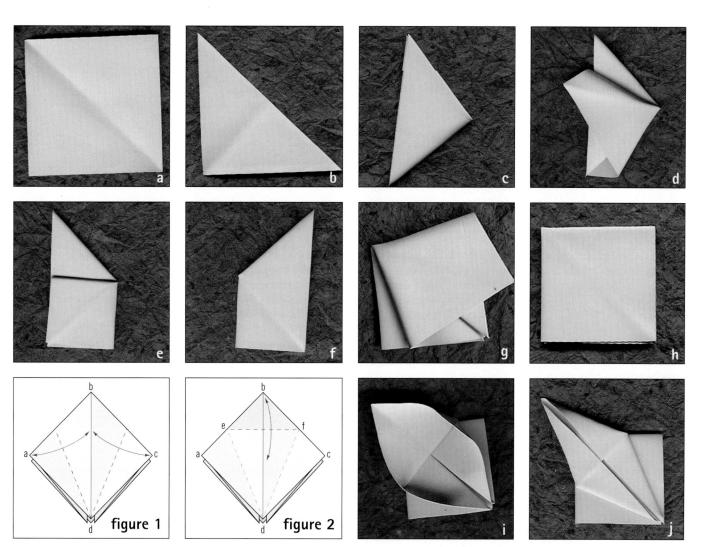

figure 1

figure 2

1 Be sure your hands and work space are dry and clean. Do not apply any olive oil or extender. If you wish, texture or type words on the sheet before using, as explained in "Typing on metal-clay sheets," page 24. Gently fold the metal-clay paper diagonally to make a triangle [a–b]. Fold again to a smaller triangle [c].

2 Now open one triangular "pocket" and refold so that it becomes a square [d–e]. Turn the piece over to the other side. Repeat—open the triangle to become a square [f–h]. (It helps if you gently flip this triangular wing to other side first.)

3 Orient the square so that the open edges face down. Follow **figure 1** and gently fold **corner a** in so that **edge a–d** is parallel to the center **line b–d**. Repeat on the other side with **corner c**. Unfold.

4 Follow **figure 2** and fold **corner b** down to make **crease e–f**. Unfold.

5 Gently open one pocket by lifting the point up [i]. Bring the sides in to the center and flatten [j].

continued on the next page

what you will need

- tools for working with metal clay, pages 11-13
- PMC+ Sheet, 2x2-inch square
- PMC+ slip
- vermiculite or alumina hydrate in a small terra-cotta saucer
- electric kiln
- vermicelli or other thin pasta
- burnishing tools, page 14
- flexible beading wire or leather cord
- crimp beads
- flatnose or crimping pliers
- wire cutters
- lobster or S-hook clasp
- assorted beads (optional)
- head pins (optional)

Before you begin, review the following sections:
- Working with metal-clay sheet or paper, page 24
- Burnishing, page 37

Working with metal-clay paper and syringe

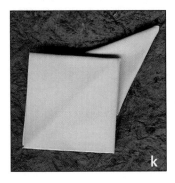

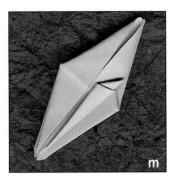

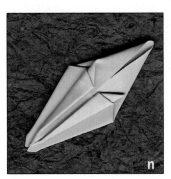

6 Turn piece over and repeat the fold on the other side [k–l]. Try to have the tips be neat and sharp since these will become the crane's wings.

7 With the "legs" (the end which splits into two) pointing down, fold each of the four edges in toward the center [m–n]. Don't worry if each leg doesn't come to an exact point. Flip to the other side and repeat.

8 To make the head and tail, bring each leg up, folding it to the inside [o–p]. Choose one leg to become the head and fold it down and to the inside [q]. Now, gently spread the wings and let the body puff out to the traditional origami crane form [r]. Reshape it slightly, if needed, so that the sharp points will not catch on your skin or clothing.

9 Fire the crane. Use an electric kiln and fire at the suggested temperature and time for PMC+. Place it in a bed of vermiculite or alumina hydrate to support the shape.

The traditional Japanese symbol of peace and long life makes for beautiful jewelry or a lasting ornament

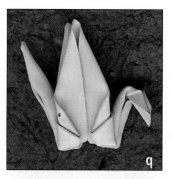

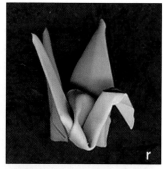

10 Do not burnish the fired crane yet. Apply a small amount of thick metal-clay slip around the center of a short piece of vermicelli or thin pasta. Attach this to the underside of the tips of the wings. Add more thick slip on the vermicelli [s].

11 Refire the crane at the recommended time and temperature for metal-clay slip. Since the crane is already fired, it does not need support this time. If you use low-fire metal-clay slip, you can use the Hot Pot kiln or a butane torch for this firing, if you wish.

12 When cool, burnish the fired crane with a brass brush. Tumble in an electric tumbler for a mirror shine or burnish with a brass brush for a satin finish. Gently rub the piece with a polishing cloth to finish.

13 String the crane by stringing the cord or beading wire through the holes left by the vermicelli [t]. String and crimp a crimp bead to hold the wires in place. Attach a clasp part to the end of each wire or cord. A lobster or S-hook clasp is best.

Earring variation

If you want to make earrings instead of a pendant, use one-fourth of a sheet. Follow steps 1-6, skip step 7, and continue with steps 8 and 9. Poke a hole through the middle of the crane with a safety pin or needle file after firing. Thread the fired crane onto a head pin, string a bead or two, and make a loop above the top bead. Open the loop of an earring wire sideways, string on the loop above the crane, and close the earring wire loop. Repeat to make the second earring.

This is a beginner-level project using pre-packaged metal-clay slip in a syringe and a sparkling cubic zirconia (CZ). Add a sterling-silver bail to hang this from a chain or glue on a tie tack to make this into a charming pin. Use the metal-clay syringe without a tip to make thick, sturdy lines. Here I made a daisy design but you could also make other shapes with the syringe. CZs are easier to work with, but if you want to use a glass cab as I have in this photo, see "Glass and metal clay," page 39, before beginning. With glass you need to use a programmable electric kiln to control the heating and cooling.

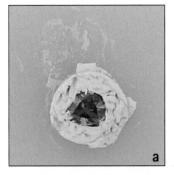

a

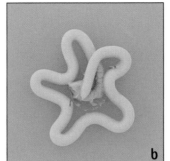

b

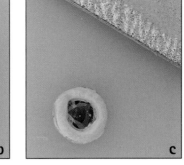

c

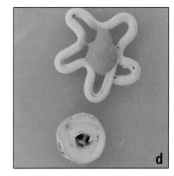

d

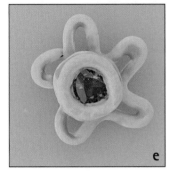

e

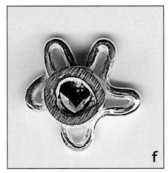

f

what you will need

- tools for working with metal clay, pages 11-13
- PMC3 or Art Clay 650 Syringe
- cubic zirconia (CZ) or small glass cabochon
- small bowl of water
- tweezers
- retractable ball point pen
- Hot Pot kiln (if using a cubic zirconia)
- electric kiln (if using a glass cab)
- burnishing tools, page 14

Before you begin, review the following sections:
- Using metal-clay syringe, page 25
- Firing with cubic zirconia, page 35
- Burnishing, page 37

Add a sparkle

of color with

cubic zirconia

1 Use a metal-clay syringe with no tip attachment to produce thick extruded clay. Have a lightly oiled sheet of plastic ready to hold the metal-clay piece. Remember to keep the tip of the syringe in the bowl of water whenever you are not using it to keep it from drying out.

2 Squeeze the syringe with a steady hand and create the bezel for the CZ. Extrude a generous amount of metal clay onto the plastic sheet. The metal clay should be thick enough to hold the CZ. Don't worry about the shape right now since it will be sanded after drying.

While the extruded clay is still moist, press the CZ into the clay using the end of a retracted ball point pen to keep the gemstone level. There should be a lip of metal clay around the CZ [a]. Add more clay from the syringe, if necessary. If there are gaps in the bezel, press the moist clay down to be sure the gemstone is secure. Let dry. Make sure the underside is also completely dried by turning the piece over after a few minutes.

3 With another small plastic sheet as a platform, use the syringe to draw a simple design in which the ends join together [b]. Turn the plastic sheet with one hand while the other hand squeezes the syringe.

4 Sand and smooth the dried bezel [c]. Use an emery board or wet/dry sandpaper to sand the top, sides, and back of the bezel. Begin with 400-grit and progress to 600-grit for a smooth finish. Using a small damp paintbrush, smooth the entire surface of the dried metal-clay piece. Let dry. Use a toothpick to remove any metal clay on the face of the CZ.

5 Attach the back of the dry, sanded bezel to the dried flower form with moist clay from the syringe [d–e]. Apply more syringe clay to the back of the flower, if necessary. Use the damp brush to smooth out any flaws on the flower. Let dry completely.

6 Fire, let cool in the kiln, burnish, and polish [f]. Attach a sterling-silver jump ring or bail to one of the petals and hang it from a fine chain. Or, if you wish to wear this as a pin, glue a tie tack finding to the back with a dab of E6000 adhesive.

Make a box from
metal-clay paper and decorate it.
The example above shows a box
decorated with metal-clay syringe only,
but you can also cut tiny designs in the
metal-clay paper to enhance the lacy effect. This
project requires two firings—one for the metal-
clay paper and another at a lower temperature for
the metal-clay syringe. The reason for this is that
it is much easier to apply the delicate metal-clay
syringe lines on the fired metal-clay sheet.
Remember to store the slip from metal-clay
syringe separately from the metal-clay
sheet scraps since they fire at
different temperatures.

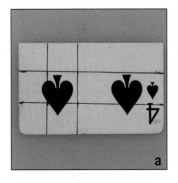

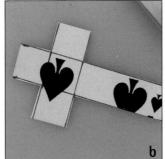

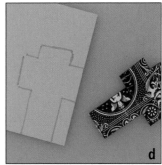

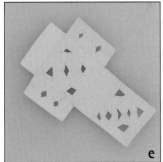

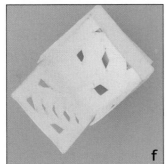

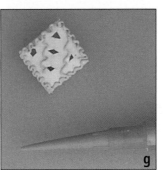

1 To make a stencil, draw a box shape on a playing card with a felt tip pen [a]. Cut it out and build a prototype [b–c]. Make adjustments as necessary.

2 Trace the stencil on the metal-clay sheet with a pencil [d]. Cut out small decorative shapes using a craft knife or small cutters, if desired [e]. To make the cuts with a craft knife, gently cut the metal-clay paper along a fold. Don't press too hard as this could cause creases to appear that could tear after firing. Avoid cutting through more than two layers. Simply refold at different angles to cut out the designs. Be careful to leave enough uncut metal-clay paper along the outside edge for decoration and support, and enough in the middle so that the shape holds together.

3 Lay the metal-clay paper flat and fire at the appropriate temperature. Metal-clay paper must be fired in an electric kiln at a high temperature. If it is fired at a lower temperature, it will be brittle and break.

Do not burnish. Use tweezers to handle the fired metal-clay paper. Carefully fold the metal clay into a box shape [f].

4 Apply the metal-clay syringe [g]. Curved lines work best as they allow for shrinkage while firing. Otherwise, the fired metal-clay sheet will buckle under the stress of the shrinking metal-clay syringe.

If you make an error (we all do!), simply rinse the fired metal-clay sheet sheet in a bowl of water and take the syringe lines off. Dry the surface and try again.

5 If you plan to hang the beads from a necklace or as earrings, add a fine-silver wire bail in one of the joints of the bead before the second firing [h].

6 Dry. To avoid handling the delicate piece, leave it on the playing card and place the card on the drying plate. Use tweezers to carefully remove the piece from the card after drying.

7 Fire at the appropriate temperature for metal-clay syringe. Place in vermiculite or on a fiber blanket for support. Burnish and polish.

---

what you will need

- PMC+ Sheet
- PMC3 Syringe
- small bowl of water
- 2 in. (5cm) 18-gauge fine-silver wire for bail (optional)
- electric kiln
- sharp scissors
- burnishing tools
- syringe tip set (optional)

Before you begin, review the following sections:
- Stencils, page 21
- Working with metal-clay sheet or paper, page 24
- Using metal-clay syringe, page 25
- Burnishing, page 37

Make lacy beads or earrings

with metal-clay paper

and syringe

Make this little house from metal-clay paper and syringe. Cut out windows and a door and decorate it with lots of spirals and swirls to achieve a sweet gingerbread house look. As in the "Lacy box bead" project, two firings are required—one for the metal-clay paper, and then a lower-temperature firing for the metal-clay syringe. Wear your house as a pin or pendant or simply enjoy it as a miniature work.

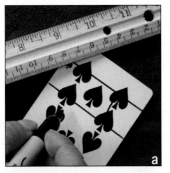

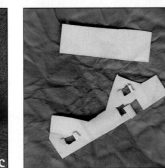

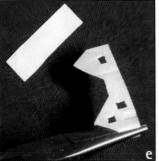

a

b

c

d

e

f

g

Make a
big impression
with this
little piece!

1 Build a prototype house out of a playing card [a–b]. Start with a simple design—a roof and four walls. Tape it together so you can see what it will look like.

2 Separate the prototype into two pieces—the roof is one piece and the four walls connected together is the other [c]. Use these pieces as a stencil.

3 Lay the stencil on the metal-clay paper and gently trace around it with a pencil. Also, mark any windows and doors you'd like to include in the design. Cut the metal-clay paper with sharp scissors [d]. Fire the two pieces flat. Fire any small metal-clay paper scraps also.

4 After the pieces have cooled, gently bend the pieces into the house shape with chainnose pliers [e–f] and add a thin layer of slip from the inside to join the walls, strengthen the corners, and join the roof to the house. The small scraps you fired earlier can be added to the inside of the house for additional support. Attach them to the middle of each wall or around windows with a small amount of metal-clay slip. Dry completely.

5 Apply the extruded clay decorations [g]. Have fun! Use curves and loops instead of straight lines. As the metal clay shrinks, the curves and loops will give and the metal-clay paper will not buckle. If you make an error when using the syringe, simply scrape off the extruded clay and drop it into a small bowl of water where it will sink to the bottom. Later you can drain off the water and keep the remaining metal clay.

6 Stand the little house on a flat surface and fire it at the low-fire metal-clay temperature. Burnish and polish. If you wish to wear this piece as a pendant, gently make holes near the top of the roof. To wear it as a pin, glue a tie tack finding on the back with E6000 adhesive.

Using organic materials with metal clay

Some of the most exciting metal clay applications involve

natural and organic materials. Leaves, flowers, and insects painted

with metal-clay slip result in beautiful fine-silver replicas of the

original items. Shells and other forms can be used as molds for

solid or hollow objects. The projects in the following chapter

represent just a few of the unlimited pieces you can make if you

let nature be your guide and inspiration. Most of the techniques

used in these projects have been covered in previous pages, but

if you need a refresher or aren't familiar with a skill, consult

Chapter 2, "Tips and techniques," before proceeding.

Capture the beauty of nature in fine silver. This pendant is made from a real leaf. The decorative cubic zirconia adds the sparkle of a dewdrop while the fine-silver wire bail looks like a tendril. Finish with a patina for a lovely natural depth in color. Choose any smooth leaf with defined veins or try flowers, pods, or other natural forms.

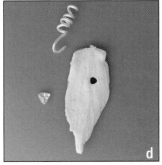

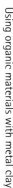

1 Prepare the two consistencies of slip before beginning. Make most of it a thick consistency, but use water to thin a small amount to flow like olive oil. Select leaves with well-defined veins and smooth surfaces. Secure the leaves to index cards by taping the stem and placing tape between the leaf and card.

2 Use a rubber-tipped clay tool to apply a layer of thin slip to the veined side of the leaf. Spread the slip to cover every line on the surface [a–b].

3 To dry the leaf, set it on a sunny windowsill for 30 minutes, or place it in a warm oven or toaster oven for 5-10 minutes.

4 Before applying the next layer, smooth the surface with a small damp makeup brush. Apply a generous layer of thick slip, taking care not to leave air pockets between layers [c]. Dry thoroughly. The leaf textures will be less visible and the surface should be smooth.

5 Apply the third layer of thick slip. Again, go over the surface with a damp brush and make sure that the edges and the area for the bail are well coated. Dry thoroughly. The surface should be completely smooth. The metal clay on the leaf should be at least three playing cards thick, especially on the edges. The leaf needs to be sturdy enough to handle. If it feels fragile at this point, apply more slip and let dry.

6 Use a pencil to mark the spots where the CZ will go. With a sanding needle or sharp X-acto knife, gently carve out a hole slightly smaller than the CZ [d]. On the back side of the leaf, dab a small amount of metal-clay slip on the edges of the hole. Use tweezers to place the CZ facedown (the flat side) on the back of the leaf. Cover the CZ with a generous amount of slip. Dry thoroughly.

7 Using fine-silver wire, make a bail with "legs." Bend and score the legs so that the metal clay can grab them. Imbed the bail legs in more slip on the backside of the leaf and dry thoroughly [e]. Gently sand the edges and the back of the leaf to smooth out the surface. Use a toothpick to remove any last particles of metal clay from the front surface of the CZ. A soft makeup brush is handy for removing the dust [f].

8 Fire in an electric kiln or Hot Pot kiln. If the leaf is not flat, support it with vermiculite or a fiber blanket. Use a bent stainless-steel wire support in the Hot Pot kiln [g]. If you are using an electric kiln, use vermiculite. Place the piece leaf side up in the kiln. The leaf will burn away, leaving just the textures. Burnish and patina. Finish with a polishing cloth to bring out the shine.

---

what you will need

- tools for working with metal clay, pages 11-13
- leaves—use ones with defined veins. Fresh or dried leaves both work. Avoid those that are hairy.
- PMC3 or Art Clay 650 Slip
- cubic zirconia
- 3 in. (7.6cm) 18-gauge fine-silver wire
- roundnose pliers
- wire cutters
- burnishing tools, page 14
- liver of sulfur
- Hot Pot kiln or electric kiln
- index cards
- pencil

Before you begin, review the following sections:
- Metal-clay slip, page 21
- Working with fine-silver wire, page 28
- Firing with cubic zirconia, page 35
- Burnishing, page 37
- Adding patina, page 37

Add dramatic

sparkle to a

natural form

Butterfly wing with gold

This project is more complex than the leaf pendant. The wing is much more fragile, and working with gold takes a little more effort. I fire first in a kiln, then use a butane torch to apply the gold. Although more steps are needed, do not be put off. This project is not difficult if you follow the directions. And the stunning results are definitely worth your time and patience.

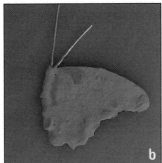

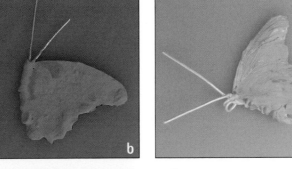

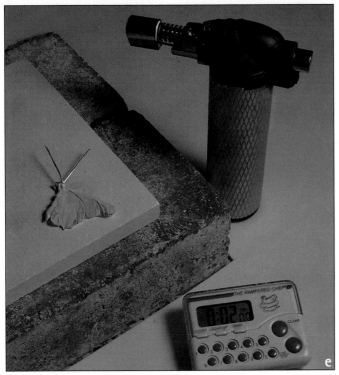

1 Begin by thinning a portion of your slip with distilled water until it is the consistency of olive oil.

2 Place a small piece of cellophane tape rolled sticky-side-out on an index card as flat as possible. Select wings with distinct veins [a]. Use tweezers to gently place the wings on the tape, textured side up.

3 Use a rubber-tipped clay tool to apply the thin slip to the wing. Spread the slip to cover the entire surface completely [b].

4 Set it on a sunny window sill for 30 minutes to dry thoroughly. If you want to speed up the drying process, place the butterfly in a warm oven or toaster oven. Usually 5-10 minutes is sufficient for the piece to dry completely. The slip should be clearly adhered to the wing and the lines will show through.

5 Before applying the next layer, go over the surface with a small damp brush. After it is dry, apply a generous layer of the thick slip, taking care not to leave air pockets between layers. Dry thoroughly. The wing textures will be less visible now and the surface should be smooth.

6 Again go over the surface with a damp brush and make sure that the edges and the area for the wire are well coated. Apply the third layer of thick slip. Dry thoroughly. The surface should be completely smooth. The metal clay should be at least three playing cards thick especially on the edges. The wing needs to be sturdy enough to handle. If it feels fragile at this point, apply more slip and let dry.

7 Cut a 3-in. piece of fine-silver wire. Wrap the center of the wire around a pair of roundnose pliers two or three times to make a bail for the pin or necklace. Angle the ends away from the loop to make the antennae. Apply some of the thick slip on the wire and then join it to the slip on the edge of the wing and dry thoroughly [c]. Gently sand the edges and the back of the wing to smooth out the surface. A soft makeup brush is handy for removing dust.

8 Fire flat with wing side up [d]. Do not burnish.

9 Now for the GOLD! Place the just-fired, clean wing with wire bail on a soldering tile [e]. Follow the directions in "Firing with a butane torch," page 32. Have the firing surface, butane torch, tweezers, water, and safety glasses ready. It may be helpful to turn the lights down so you can see the colors of the metal clay during firing.

continued on the next page

---

what you will need

- tools for working with metals clay, pages 11-13
- butterfly wings - use ones with defined veins
- PMC3 or Art Clay 650 Slip
- Aura 22 or pure gold sheet Aura 22
- fine tip brush for gold work
- 3 in. (7.6cm) 18-gauge fine-silver wire (for bail, antenna)
- roundnose pliers
- wire cutters
- Hot Pot kiln or electric kiln
- butane torch and torching setup (see page 32)
- cellophane tape
- blue gel school glue
- index card
- burnishing tools, page 14
- liver of sulfur
- sterling silver stick pin
- beads (optional)

Before you begin, review the following sections:
- Metal-clay slip, page 21
- Working with fine-silver wire, page 28
- Burnishing, page 37
- Adding patina, page 37
- Easing into gold, page 40

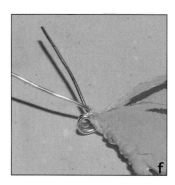

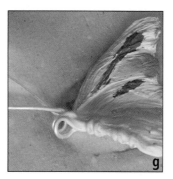

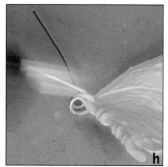

10 Read "Easing into gold," page 40, before applying gold. Tack the gold sheet down with a small amount of blue gel glue. If you are new to torch firing, try torch firing a small silver metal clay piece. Learn to recognize the fusing process when the metal is glowing a reddish orange color and the melting point when the metal will begin to shine.

11 Apply one thin layer of Aura 22 or gold sheet with each firing [f]. Do not apply thick layers as they are more likely to peel off. You can always stop, let the piece air cool, and see how it looks. While the piece is hot, use a hard burnishing tool to press gold onto silver. Then continue if the gold does not look securely adhered to the silver. Apply one layer of the gold paste with each firing to deepen the gold color [g-i].

12 You can burnish and polish the fired piece just as you would silver metal clay. A patina may bring out the contrast between the silver and gold. Only the silver takes on the patina. Finish with a polishing cloth to bring out the shine. Attach beads to the end of the antennae with glue. Slide the butterfly onto a stick pin finding or a chain to make a necklace.

13 If you wish to make a necklace like the one below, make two butterfly wing units. Before firing, make tiny holes in the wing tips. Make four beaded dangles on wire head pins and attach the dangles to the fired and burnished wings. String a large bead between the two wings and finish the necklace as desired.

Apply a gorgeous touch of 22K gold on a butterfly wing

Add a personal touch to a clock by molding hands with silver clay. Attach the molded silver forms directly onto the clock hands. Here I used a store-bought clock that I took apart. I then covered the original face with handmade paper. You could also purchase just the clock motor and hands and make your own clock case. Think of the possibilities . . . a piece of polished wood or stone, a pretty box, or a framed photo would make a very special, original, and personal clock face.

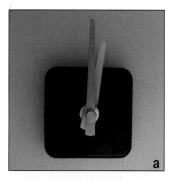

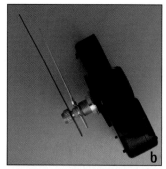

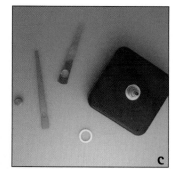

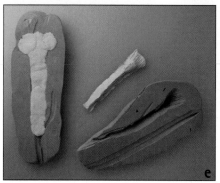

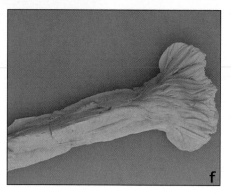

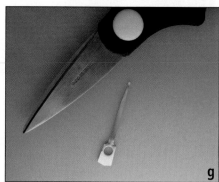

1 Use a clock with stainless steel or brass hands [a]. If you are not sure what they're made of, try firing one clock hand by itself at the temperature you will use for the metal clay you have. If it survives one firing it will work. Do not worry if it changes color. Make a note of the amount of space between the two clock hands [b]. You will need to keep the silver hands thin enough to fit into this space. Take the clock apart [c] and keep all the clock parts in a sealable plastic bag.

2 To make the mold, begin by selecting two or three flowers, leaves, or stems to use for the hands [d]. Hold them against the clock hands to see that they will be the right length. You can trim the clock hands down if necessary. In this case I used a flower and a leaf. Using double-sided tape or white glue, gently press the flower and leaf, texture-side up, on a plastic sheet so that they lay flat and straight. Mix the molding compound and press it on top of the flower and leaf. Let it cure for the amount of time recommended by the manufacturer. Release the forms from the molds.

3 For this project, I used Art Clay Slow Dry so that the delicate flower and leaf shapes could be adjusted before the clay dried. Press the moist metal clay into the molds firmly to capture the fine details of the flower and leaf. Flex the mold to pop the moist clay forms out of the mold [e].

what you will need

- tools for working with metal clay, pages 11-13
- clock or clock motor with stainless-steel or brass hands
- Art Clay Slow Dry
- Art Clay 650 slip
- small fresh flowers, leaves, or stems
- double-sided tape or white glue
- heavy duty scissors
- electric kiln
- burnishing tools, page 14
- liver of sulfur
- two-part silicon molding compound
- handmade papers to make clock face (optional)

Before you begin, review the following sections:
- Making a mold, page 28
- Carving and sanding metal clay, page 30
- Burnishing, page 37
- Adding patina, page 37

4 Lay the moist metal clay forms on a flat surface to dry. Adjust the clay forms so that they are straight and flat [f]. Art Clay Slow Dry will require more time to dry completely; see the instructions in the package.

5 Sand and trim the dried metal clay forms. Use an emery board to sand the sides straight. Use needle files to sand the flower petals. If the metal clay form is too thick (consult the measurement you took in step 1), sand extra clay off the back side of the hands.

6 Place the metal clay forms on the clock hands. The metal clay should cover the clock hands, so trim the hands with heavy-duty scissors if needed [g].

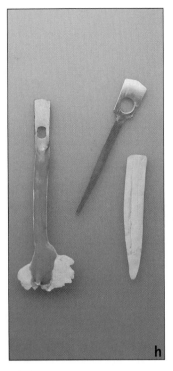

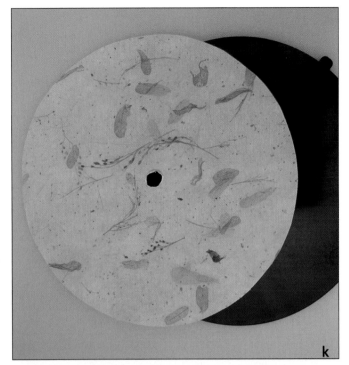

k

h

j

7 Fire the metal clay forms at 1470°F (800°C) for 30 minutes. Do not burnish.

8 Attach the fired forms to the clock hands. Again, trim the metal clock hands if needed. Remember to leave some space around the holes for the screws [h]. Use a generous amount of the thick metal-clay slip to attach the metal-clay forms to the clock hands. Dry completely.

9 Sand the dried clock hands. Try attaching them to the clock motor [i]. If they don't fit properly, sand again. Fire the clock hands at the appropriate temperature for the metal-clay slip you are using.

10 Burnish, add a liver or sulfur patina, and polish [j]. The fine details of the flower should show up very clearly. If you wish to customize your clock face, do it now. Here I simply traced the original face onto handmade paper and cut it out [k]. I attached it to a layer of white paper and then glued it onto the original face. Now put your mechanical skills to the test and put the clock back together. I wanted to hide the screw and metal hand ends in the center of the clock [l], so I covered them with a round piece of paper (see page 113).

l

Make your own hands
of time with fine silver

Shell pendant

You can use a two-part silicon molding compound to make a fabulous pendant from a real shell. Use your carving skills to reduce the weight and make it a hollow piece. The key to success for this project is proper drying. By drying from the outside in, the external surface hardens and holds its shape and texture while the internal surface remains moist enough for carving.

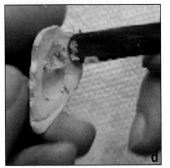

1. Select a shell with clear lines and a space for making the hole where the bail can be added. Mark halfway points on the sides of the shell with a felt-tip pen.

2. To capture the complete shape of the shell, you will make a mold that has two parts; each section will contain half of the shell. Mix equal parts of the two-part silicon molding compound and press the shell halfway into it up to the marked points [a]. Allow the silicon to cure according to the manufacturer's instructions. Remove the mold for the first half. Mix another batch of molding compound and press the opposite side of the shell halfway into the compound up to the marked points. Allow it to cure. Remove the mold and trim to remove any imperfections [b].

3. Press the metal clay into each of the two molds. Immediately remove the clay pieces and place them on a playing card or plastic sheet [c].

4. Quickly texture the clay with a leather punch or rubber stamp by gently pressing the texture item into the moist clay. Dry the pieces texture-side up for a few minutes in a warm oven. Be careful not to overheat or burn the clay.

5. Holding one half of the shell, gently carve out the moist clay inside the shell [d]. Keep the shell walls a consistent thickness.

6. Use an X-acto knife or a small push-drill bit to make the hole for the bail to go through [e]. Join the two shell halves together using thick slip. Smooth the seams and edges [f]. Dry again in the warm oven until the clay is bone dry. Sand the edges smooth with needle files.

7. Support the clay shell in vermiculite if firing in an electric kiln or on a wire rack if using the Hot Pot kiln. Fire, burnish, and finish as desired. Slide the pendant onto a bail and enjoy.

For something a little different, use this technique to make a perfume bottle [g]. I added a small cylinder at the top to form the neck of the bottle and added bead dangles and a beaded wire stopper.

what you will need

- tools for working with metal clay, pages 11-13
- PMC3 or Art Clay 650
- PMC3 or Art Clay 650 slip
- shell
- two-part silicon molding compound
- leather punches or rubber stamps
- sterling silver bail or 2 in. (5cm) 18-gauge fine-silver wire
- Hot Pot kiln or electric kiln
- warm oven
- burnishing tools, page 14
- small push drill and bit
- liver of sulfur (optional)

Before you begin, review the following sections:
- Hollow forms, page 25
- Making a mold, page 28
- Burnishing, page 37
- Adding patina, page 37

Make this beautiful pendant with two molds of a real shell

Using organic materials with metal clay

Pendant slide by Hattie Sanderson, Speedy Peacock photo.

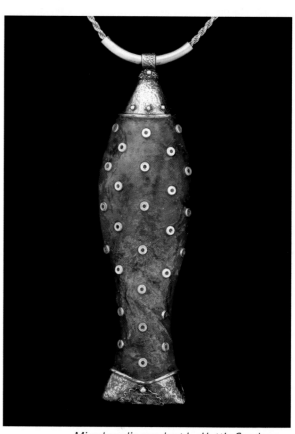

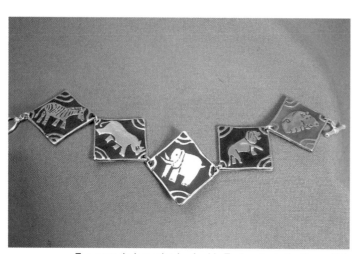

Zoo parade bracelet by Jackie Truty, photo by the artist.

Mixed media pendant by Hattie Sanderson, Speedy Peacock photo.

Inspiration

See what artisans around the country are creating with metal clay!

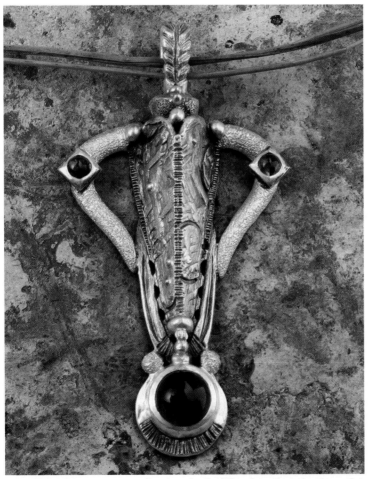

Pendant by Carl Stanley, photo by the artist.

Pendant by Jackie Truty, photo by the artist.

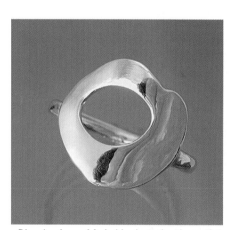

Ring by Anna M. Aoki, photo by the artist.

*Pendant by Jackie Truty,
photo by the artist.*

Pin by Jackie Truty, photo by the artist.

Lidded pendant by Jackie Truty, photo by the artist.

Rings by Anna M. Aoki,
photo by the artist.

Enamelled pendant by Carl Stanley, photo by the artist.

Sakura necklace by Anna M. Aoki,
photo by the artist.

*Ring by Hattie Sanderson,
Speedy Peacock photo.*

*Gingko earrings by Nana Mizushima,
photo by the artist.*

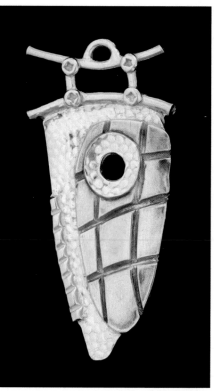

*Pendant by Hattie Sanderson,
Speedy Peacock photo.*

Mixed media pin by Carl Stanley, photo by the artist.

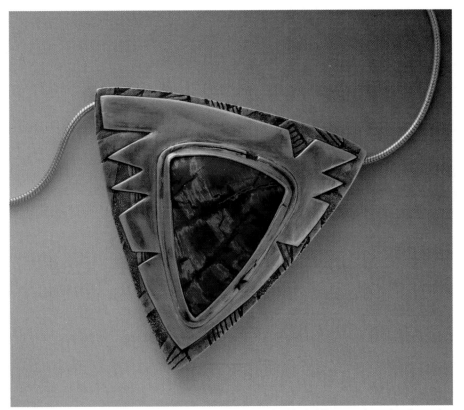

Pendant with tabu jasper stone by Linda Warner, photo by the artist.

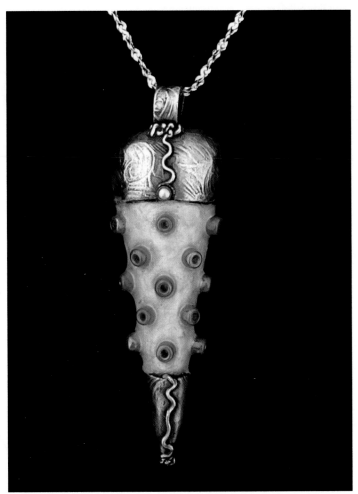

Metal clay beads by Linda Warner, photo by the artist.

Mixed media pendant by Hattie Sanderson, Speedy Peacock photo.

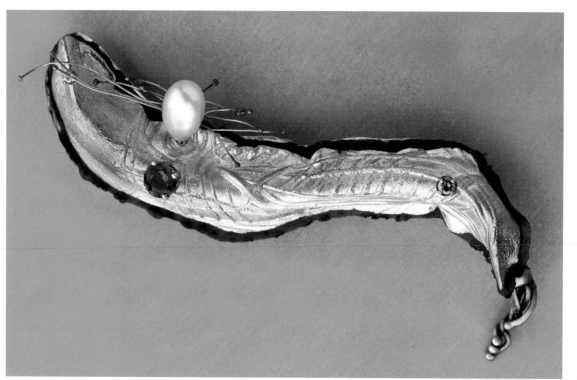

Mixed media brooch by Carl Stanley, photo by the artist.

*Hollow bi-dome earrings
by Carl Stanley,
photo by the artist.*

Daisy pendant by Jennifer J. MacLean, Vintage Artifacts photo.

Resources and suppliers

Information web sites

Art Clay Silver
www.artclay.com.jp/htm/what.html
Find information on the Art Clay brand of metal clay.

Art Clay World USA
www.artclayworld.com/
Supplier of Art Clay products, classes, and information.

Art Jewelry Magazine forum
www.artjewelrymag.com/art/
community/forum
Questions and answers on jewelry making and metal clay.

Juried Show of PMC work
www.artisanscenterofvirginia.org/
exhibitions/PMC/index_3.htm
Be inspired! Nana's pieces are in the center photo of a starfish necklace and two bracelets.

Metal Clay Artists
www.lapidaryjournal.com/feature/
featsofclay.com
An article on current work.

Metal Clay Gallery
http://groups.yahoo.com/group/metalclay/
Useful information through a question-and-answer site.

Metal Clay Web Ring
http://c.webring.com/hub?ring=
metalclaywebring
Forum and web sites on metal clay.

Precious_Metal_Clay_IL-WI
http://groups.yahoo.com/group/Precious_
Metal_Clay_IL-WI/
Email list for the professional artist or hobbyist interested in learning about and sharing information regarding Precious Metal Clay.

PMC Guild
www.pmcguild.com
Membership organization with newsletter, information on PMC classes throughout the country, and technical tips.

The Enamelist Society
www.enamelistsociety.org/
Information about glass enameling.

National Polymer Clay Guild
www.npcg.org/
Information on polymer clay, classes, and local guilds.

The Bead Bugle
www.nfobase.com/html/moldable_metal_
clay.html
On-line article on metal clay.

Tonnbo Design
www.nanajewelry.com/ or
www.tonnbodesign.com/
Examples of PMC work by Nana V. Mizushima. PMC classes, information, and basic supplies.

Society of American Silversmiths
www.silversmithing.com/1clay.htm
An article introducing PMC. Most of the information is also applicable to Art Clay.

Suppliers of metal clay and related products

Art Clay World USA
www.artclayworld.com/
Supplier of Art Clay products, classes, and information.

Delphi Glass Supply
www.delphiglass.com/
Glass and jewelry-making classes and supplies.

Glass Orchids
www.glassorchids.com/
Dichroic glass and supplies.

Paragon Kilns
www.paragonweb.com/
Manufacturers of electric kilns.

PMC Connection
www.pmcconnection.com/
Supplies, tools, and certification classes.

PMC Supply.com
www.pmcsupply.com/shop.html
PMC supplies and tools.

Rio Grande
www.riogrande.com/PMC/index.htm
A large jewelry supply company with a complete line of jewelry making tools and supplies.

Santa Fe Jewelry Supply
www.sfjssantafe.com/
Jewelry findings, tools, and beads.

Sarajane's Polyclay Gallery
www.polyclay.com/
Examples of polymer clay art.

Silver Clay
www.silver-clay.com/
Art Clay and PMC supplies and information. Based in New Mexico.

Whole Lotta Whimsy
www.wholelottawhimsy.com/
The on-line extension of their Arizona-based store. PMC supplies, tools, and classes.

Suggested reading

Magazines: Visit your local library to browse back issues.

Art Jewelry magazine: stunning examples of metal clay work.

Bead&Button magazine: offers step-by-step instructions on jewelry projects.

Beadwork magazine: lots of ideas on combining your creations with beadwork.

Belle Armoire magazine: gorgeous photos of jewelry and "wearable art" projects.

Jewelry Crafts magazine: many articles on metal clay work.

Lapidary Journal: magazine often contains articles on metal clay.

Books: Find books by looking under metal clay, silver clay or Precious Metal Clay.

The Art of Metal Clay—Techniques for Creating Jewelry and Decorative Objects by Sherri Haab. Published by Watson Guptill Publications, 2003.

Creative Metal Clay Jewelry—Techniques, Projects, Inspiration by CeCe Wire. Published by Lark Books, 2003.

Art Clay Silver & Gold—18 Unique Jewelry Pieces to Make in a Day by Jackie Truty. Published by Krause Publications, 2003.

Contributor information

Arleen Alleman
Owner/artist, A Alleman Jewelry Art
web site: www.aallemanjewelry.com
email: arleen@aol.com

Anna M. Aoki
Freelance artist
web site: www10.plala.or.jp/daini/

Sally Evans
Owner/artist, Evans & Evans Studios
P.O. Box 3801
Englewood, CO 80155
phone: (303) 792-5651
web site: www.sallyevansart.com
email: sally@sallyevansart.com

Hattie Sanderson
Owner/artist, Hattie Sanderson Art Studio
Clare, IL
phone: (815) 393-4365
email: hatsan@netzetro.net

Carl Stanley
Owner/artist, Carl Stanley Jewelry Arts
1744 Calle Poniente
Santa Barbara,CA 93101
web site: carlstanleyjewelryarts.com
email: carl@carlstanleyjewelryarts.com
phone: (805) 687-5415
fax: (805) 687-3215

Jackie Truty
Master instructor, Art Clay World
4535 Southwest Highway
Oaklawn, IL 60435
web site: www.artclayworld.com
email: jackie@artclayworld.com
phone: (708) 857-8800
fax: (708) 636-5408

Glossary

annealing A process used when firing with glass. Controlling the cooling of hot glass to prevent cracks and breaks.

bail A wire loop or shaped piece of metal used to hang a pendant or charm on a chain or necklace.

bezel Traditionally a bezel is a thin strip of metal used to hold a gem or stone. In this book, it refers to any metal clay form that holds a decorative stone.

binder The material mixed together with particles of silver or gold to create metal clay. It is burned out during the firing process.

bisque Unglazed porcelain or ceramics that has been fired.

bone-dry Unfired metal clay that is completely dry, also known as greenware.

burnish To bring out the shine of fired metal clay by compressing the surface with a tool.

butane torch A small handheld torch which uses the same fuel used in lighters. Available in hardware and cooking stores.

cabochon A stone, glass, or other material shaped to fit into a metal bezel on a piece of jewelry. Usually flat on one side and rounded on the other.

cold molding compound Also known as two-part silicone molding compound. Unlike the molds made with heat, this compound works at room temperature with the chemical reaction of two formulas mixed together.

core Refers to the material used to support the inside of a hollow form. Coreless forms are small hollow metal-clay forms, which do not require a core.

crash cool A technique used when firing glass, particularly dichroic glass, to prevent the clouding and weakening of glass.

CZ (cubic zirconia) A man-made gemstone that resembles a diamond. Unlike diamonds, CZs can withstand the heat of firing with metal clay.

dichroic glass A type of glass with beautiful layers of iridescent colors. This effect is caused by a layer of metallic oxide in the glass.

extender A solution that is added to metal clay to maintain its moisture content. Distilled water with glycerin is one formula.

extruded metal clay Thin strips of metal clay produced by the metal-clay syringe.

fine silver .999 silver or pure silver, marked as 999 or FS on jewelry. Fine silver is softer than sterling silver but it does not tarnish as quickly as sterling. Metal clay fires to become fine silver.

fire scale An unsightly stain that occurs when sterling silver is fired or soldered. Caused by oxygen combining with copper in the sterling silver. Does not occur with fine silver.

fusing The act of joining metals through heat and/or pressure.

girdle The widest part of a gemstone.

greenware Unfired bone-dry metal clay.

hallmark A mark stamped onto jewelry that shows the type of metal used.

Keum-Boo A technique for applying gold to fired metal clay, based on an ancient Korean metalworking method.

kiln An oven-type equipment used to fire metal clay

leather-hard Unfired metal clay that is not completely dry. It will feel clammy and cool to the touch.

liver of sulfur Potassa sulphurata. A chemical used to give metal a rich, aged appearance. *See also* patina.

low-temperature firing metal clay These metal clays fire at a lower temperature than the original metal-clay formulas. Low-fire metal clays include PMC+, PMC3 and Art Clay 650.

metal clay The generic term most commonly used. Precious Metal Clay (PMC) refers to products produced by Mitsubishi Materials. Art Clay refers to products produced by Aida Chemical Industries. Also known as silver clay.

metal-clay paper The generic term for a particular product that is different from the clay form. This product is known as either Art Clay Silver Paper Type or PMC+ Sheet. Metal-clay paper resembles handmade paper.

metal-clay syringe Metal clay that has been thinned with water and packaged in ready-to-use syringes.

origami The traditional Japanese craft of folding paper.

oxidizing The unsightly darkening of some metals, like sterling silver, that occurs during firing or torching.

patina A treatment of metal used to create an antique or colored finish. Liver of sulfur is a commonly used patina.

programmable electric kiln Kiln which can be programmed to reach different temperatures, hold that temperature for different amounts of time, and heat/cool at different speeds (ramping).

quench To immediately cool hot metal by dipping it into water.

rehydrating Adding water to dried, unfired metal clay to bring it back to moist clay condition.

ring mandrel A slightly tapered wooden cone on which rings can be formed. A mandrel can also be made with paper, though wood is preferable for use with metal clay.

rubber block A nonslip support platform which can hold the project being worked on. This enables the project to be turned without handling the piece directly.

sandwich method This is a bead-making technique I devised to make hollow beads without using a bead core.

satin finish A soft sheen finish on fired metal clay. A soft brass brush works well to achieve this finish.

shim A tool used to help roll metal clay to a consistent thickness. Two stacks of playing cards, a mat board, or a foam rubber craft sheet cut into a frame are all possible choices for making a shim. By keeping the roller ends on the shim, the metal clay will be an even thickness.

slip Unfired metal clay softened with water. Also called paste. Thin slip should be the consistency of lotion while thick slip should be more like face cream.

snakes Smooth, round strips rolled out using a Plexiglas sheet or plastic lid.

sintering The fusing together of metal clay particles during firing. Silver sinters at 1650°F (900°C); gold sinters at 1830°F (1000°C).

sterling silver .95 silver. An alloy of 95 percent fine silver and 5 percent copper or other metals.

tumbler A small machine used to burnish fired metal-clay pieces. It continuously rolls a container holding stainless-steel shot and a burnishing compound. Also known as a rock tumbler.

Index